Success University for Women™

Wisdom Working for YOU!

Created by

Jan Fraser and Cather...

written by successful women from around the world

D1114485

Copyright© 2015 by Success University for Women™*, LLC*

All rights reserved under the Pan-American and International Copyright Conventions.

This book may not be reproduced, in whole or in part, in any form or by any means electronic or mechanical, including photocopying, recording, or by any information storage and retrieval system now known or hereafter invented, without written permission from the publisher, *Success University for Women*™*, LLC,* except in the case of brief quotations embodied in critical reviews and certain other non-commercial uses permitted by copyright law.

Throughout this book, registered trademarks are the property of their respective companies.

Success University for Women™ *– Wisdom Working for You*
Volume 1
Library of Congress Cataloging-in-Publication Date available upon request
ISBN-13: 978-0-9801104-5-6 | ISBN-10: 0-9801104-5-9
Publishers: *Success University for Women*™*, LLC*

Designed by Helen Scarth, Stuf² Incorporated (*www.stuf2.com*)
Manuscript Edited by Kathryn Marion (*www.kathrynmarion.com*)

To order this title, please visit:
www.successuniversityforwomen.com

To bring a Success University for Women conference or speaker to your area, please email *info@successuniversityforwomen.com*

Praise for Success University for Women™

"This book is a MUST READ for women moving through the tough challenges of navigating a successful career or business. The phenomenal authors of *Success University for Women*™ have experienced tragedy, failure, unimaginable losses—and each found a way through the darkness into the light. Grab hold of this lifeline! It will be the most empowering, motivating thing you'll do all year."

*Teresa de Grosbois, International best-selling Author of **Mass Influence – the habits of the highly influential** and Founder, Evolutionary Business Council*

"If you're a woman, you need this book! If you're a man, you'd be wise buy it for your wife, daughter, sisters. Twenty-four amazing women have shared their life success stories to make your life better. This book is full of wisdom, inspiration, and suggestions that will stir your heart and spur you on to action in whatever endeavor you are engaged, even if it is just LIFE!"

Sally Huss, Amazon Best-Selling Children's Books Author

"You have a vision. But you won't get far without the skills and tools to make it a reality. *Success University for Women*™ will open the door to your potential and the world of possibility that lies beyond. The rest is up to you."

Susan Macaulay
Creator & Curator of Amazing Women Rock.com

"As an early bird in the women's movement, now at 85, I can say that this book tells the story brilliantly of what we can do to fulfill our own magnificent destinies at a time when the world

Praise for Success University for Women™

is in deep need of feminine co-creativity and genius. Bravo to all of us!"

Barbara Marx Hubbard, Foundation of Conscious Evolution

"*Success University for Women*™ demonstrates the importance of women. Their values, their different points of view, their patience, effort, constancy...and how wonderful it will be if women join their intelligence to change the world. As Margaret Thatcher said, 'Being powerful is like being a lady. If you have to tell people you are, you aren't'."

Mayte Domingo, CEO Hospitality Sport, Spain

"Whether you are a new professional or entrepreneur, just embarking on your personal (and business) journey; or a woman navigating challenging transitions in her work and home life; or an over-achiever now looking for more fulfillment and success, this book is an inspirational roadmap for all women."

Marie Warner, CEO & Founder, Boston Women Connect

"This book demonstrates that the power that is within us is greater that the power that is around us. It contains moving stories of remarkable women who have defied all odds to achieve the highest of their dreams."

Roselyn Mkweza-Thupa, Head, Commercial Banking, Standard Bank Malawi

"I've been helping women find themselves for over 35 years as a psychotherapist, educator and originator of the ground-

Praise for Success University for Women™

breaking RIM Method, an inventive way to tap your emotional operating system for better health. Having worked alongside many of these women, I know their intention is to support and uplift YOU. Read their stories, follow their strategies, find your new path. I was truly inspired by this book—I know you will be, too."

Deb Sandella, Ph.D., M.A., R.N., Award-winning Author and Founder of The RIM Institute

"As the Dalai Lama said, 'The world will be saved by the Western woman.' This famous quote from the leader of Tibetan Buddhism points to the power of conscious, financially secure women to lead the way in uplifting the collective consciousness of humanity. The contributing authors of *Success University for Women*™, regardless of whether they live in the East or in the West, offer deep wisdom and clear guidance to those who are yearning for a sense of purpose, fulfillment, and meaning in their lives and are committed to taking loving care of all life on the planet."

*Carolyn Anderson, Co-Founder of Global Family and Hummingbird Community, Co-Author of **The Co-Creator's Handbook***

Success University for Women™

Created by Jan Fraser and Catherine Scheers

Contributing Authors
(In Alphabetical Order)

J.L. (Jani) Ashmore
Amanda Brown
Sharon Cahir
Anastasia Davidova
Beth Gardner
Michelle Garnier-Chedotal
Lourdes Carmona Gutiérrez
Jan Fraser
Lori Harder
Trisha Jacobson
Mayra Llado
Amina Mahkdoom
Estelle Nuka
Danne Reed
Jean Ann Reuter
Jennie Ritchie
Caroline Rochon
Anita Sanchez
Catherine Scheers
Carol Talbot
Jacqueline Throop-Robinson
Susan Treadgold
Lotte Vesterli
Carla White

Success University for Women™

Disclaimer

Founded in 2015 by Jan Fraser and Catherine Scheers, *Success University for Women*™ is a company whose mission is to empower and educate women around the world through our books, conferences, and online courses.

This book shares the lessons of the 'school of hard-knocks' of the authors—lessons learned the hard way, through life, through mistakes, by searching for answers, reading books, taking courses, finding mentors, learning a better way. We are honored to share their stories with you.

The stories you are about to read are each author's personal story and opinion. Any sharing of personal information or names is at their discretion. Their struggles and their victories are their unique experiences. We make no claims that you will experience exactly the same results.

Success University for Women™ is not a post-secondary institution. While we do offer training, workshops, and conferences to empower and educate women, and a link to your *Certificate of Completion* at the end of this book, we do not promise you a two or four year university degree.

May you find inspiration and motivation in these stories to uplift and encourage you, and direct your path.

Contents

Contents

Contents

Dedication

T his book is dedicated to the many women who have gone before us, lighting the path for women in business throughout the world. It's for our mothers, grandmothers, and ancestors who taught us the qualities that will be shared in this book. It's for the women in our lives—daughters, sisters, nieces, friends, and fabulous co-authors, who inspired and encouraged us each step of the way. We hope you will see the love we feel for you reflected back in this book.

*May you find the secret to your success
in these pages.*

Jan Fraser   Catherine Scheers

Co-Founders, *Success University for Women*™

Acknowledgements

*T*his book could not have taken shape without the love and trust that these co-authors placed in our hands. Thank you for never losing sight of our mission to encourage women throughout the world.

To our mentor, Jack Canfield—thank you for believing in us and this project and writing the foreword for this book. But more than that—your principles are reflected in so many of these pages, and in our lives. Thank you for your continual encouragement and support.

Many thanks to our talented designer, Helen Scarth. She has the patience of Job, and is incredibly talented in turning our thoughts into reality. Thanks also to our intrepid editor Kathryn Marion.

Lastly and by no means least, thank you to our stalwart husbands Ian and Chris who held down the fort while we were off trying to create not just a book, but a movement. They believed us when we said it wouldn't take much time in between running our lives and businesses, even though they probably knew better than we did what a great undertaking this would be. For your guidance, hand-holding, wet shoulders and unconditional love, we cannot thank you enough.

Foreword

Jack Canfield

Known as America's #1 Success Coach, Jack Canfield is the CEO of the Canfield Training Group in Santa Barbara, California. He trains and coaches entrepreneurs, corporate leaders, managers, sales professionals, and the general public in how to accelerate the achievement of their personal, professional and financial goals.

Jack is best known as the co-author of the #1 New York Times best-selling *Chicken Soup for the Soul*® book series, which has sold more than 500 million books in 47 languages, including 11 New York Times #1 best-sellers.

His other books include **The Success Principles**™: *How to Get from Where You Are to Where You Want to Be* (recently revised as the 10th Anniversary Edition)*; The Success Principles for Teens; The Aladdin Factor; Dare to Win; Heart at Work; The Power of Focus: How to Hit Your Personal, Financial and Business Goals with Absolute*

Confidence and Certainty; You've Got to Read This Book; Tapping into Ultimate Success; Jack Canfield's Key to Living the Law of Attraction: A Simple Guide to Creating the Life of Your Dreams; and his recent novel—*The Golden Motorcycle Gang: A Story of Transformation.*

Jack is a dynamic speaker and was recently inducted into the National Speakers Association's Speakers Hall of Fame. He has appeared on more than 1,000 radio and television shows including Oprah, Montel, Larry King Live, the Today Show, Fox and Friends, and two hour-long PBS Specials devoted exclusively to his work.

Jack is also a featured teacher in 12 movies including *The Secret, The Meta-Secret, The Truth, The Keeper of the Keys, Tapping into the Source,* and *The Tapping Solution.*

He is the Founder of the Transformational Leadership Council and a member of Evolutionary Leaders, two groups devoted to helping create a world that works for everyone.

Jack is a graduate of Harvard, earned his M.Ed. from the University of Massachusetts, and has received three honorary doctorates in psychology and public service. He is married, has three children, two step-children and a grandson.

For more information visit:
www.JackCanfield.com

Foreword

by Jack Canfield

*T*he empowerment of women is one of the most important initiatives at this time in our history, and it has been an important focus of my work for the past 10 years. Two of the people who have supported me the most in that work are Jan Fraser and Catherine Scheers, the editors and compilers of this wonderful book you are holding in your hands. When I declared my intention to train one million trainers to bring this empowerment work to the world by teaching the principles and techniques from my book *The Success Principles*™ in the form of interactive, experiential workshops, they were among the first people to step up and say, "I'm in!"

Now they have gone one step further by compiling this book of inspiring and empowering stories of women who have had the courage to stand up, show up, grow up, and pursue their most heartfelt passions. And I'm so excited because all of the women whose stories you will read are also part of this new movement to empower and transform the world through this movement of dedicated, committed, competent women *Success Principles*™ Trainers. I'm excited because I have watched them face and transcend their fears, self-doubts, limiting beliefs, and real world obstacles and roadblocks, and create success and magic in all areas of their lives due to their commitment to be of greater service to themselves, their families, their businesses and their communities.

These speakers, trainers, coaches, counselors and mentors have created a book that will take you through the process of achieving all your most important goals, whether or not you have graduated from an accredited university or the "university of life." What you will learn in these pages are things you will never learn even in the most esteemed universities—the seldom-taught curriculum of the principles and strategies that are absolutely necessary to create the personal and professional life of your dreams.

What makes this book so readable is that all of this is presented in the form of their real-life stories, and as you know from my *Chicken Soup for the Soul*® series, stories capture the emotions underneath the concept and Velcro it to your mind.

The courageous women in this book pull back the curtain and share their joys, sorrows, fears and triumphs, insights and wisdom to help you understand and apply these success principles in your life so you can quickly soar to wherever you want to be. This book is full of shared and loving wisdom to support you.

No matter whether you are looking for support for your personal or your professional life, I promise you will find it inside this book.

I wish you great joy on your journey to success.

Jack Canfield

Preface

PREFACE

*A*re you feeling stuck in any area of your life? Are you restless and searching for a different path to success? Then you've come to the right place. You are about to meet 24 spectacular women who have been where you are standing, and they found a way to success—each in their own way. They are here to show you how *they did it* and how *you can, too!*

These authors are as different from each other as night is from day—some are younger, some more seasoned; some are introverts, others extroverts; they are career women, stay-at-home moms, and entrepreneurs; they are mothers, grandmothers, and women without children. They've faced losses and they've had victories. Their occupations differ wildly; they reside all around the world; their ages range from the 20's to the 60's. Yet they have encountered similar struggles—struggles with health, love, careers, money, family—and sometimes several of these at once! You will see your own challenges reflected in their stories. They each found a different way out, through, or around their problems.

About this Book

Success University for Women™ *- Wisdom Working for You* is divided into four sections for ease in navigation.

Section 1 is *Sourcing Success,* for those who are just starting out in their career, switching careers, or entering a new chapter in their lives. These authors will encourage you; their stories will strengthen your determination.

PREFACE

Section 2 is *Striving for Success.* This section contains the stories of ambitious women from around the world who were determined to find a way through their challenges to succeed.

Section 3 is *Smoothing Success.* On the road to success, life happens; the unexpected occurs and we must be prepared to handle it and keep going. These women met life head-on and became more in the process.

Section 4 is *Soaring in Success.* These authors demonstrate that success takes stamina, constant evolving, learning to dance with life using grace and courage, and staying connected to the true source of wisdom.

You will see common threads throughout the book and several themes with which most women can relate.

At the end of each chapter, you'll find that author's *Success University for Women*™ *Success Strategies.* These *Success Strategies* summarize their chapter and give you words of wisdom to guide you on your journey. Comprehensive exercises for every chapter can be found in our *Success University for Women*™ *- Wisdom Working for You Companion Workbook, Volume 1.* Please visit *www.successuniversityforwomen.com* for your copy.

After you have read these stories, and incorporated this 'curriculum' into your own life, you will be ready to graduate from *Success University for Women*™. All convocations come with a Graduation Certificate—you will find a link to yours at the end of this book.

Section 1

Sourcing Success

SECTION 1: INTRODUCTION

*W*hether you are new to the business world, beginning a new chapter in your life, or need a good, swift kick in your determination, this section is for you. *Sourcing Success* refers to finding the direction, tools, and focus you need to succeed.

Your teachers for this course hail from seven countries, three continents, and speak four languages. They are all successful in their own right and have stood where you now stand: at a new beginning, a fresh start.

International Speaker and French-Canadian Television Personality *Caroline Rochon* bravely chose to focus on clarity after a traumatic event in her life. *Lourdes Carmona Gutiérrez* from Spain was struck by similar clarity early in life and chose to believe in her dream, despite the obstacles to becoming a Commercial Airline Pilot.

Estelle Nuka persisted in her determination to become one of the few Chartered Accountants in Malawi, even after a tragic, heart-breaking loss. Fitness Cover Model *Lori Harder* from the United States exemplifies the discipline required for personal and professional success, while the UK's *Susan Treadgold* shares one of the best-kept secrets of success: Energy. But success without staying true to oneself is hollow—America teacher *Trisha Jacobson* is a role model for authenticity.

May you find within their compelling stories the wisdom, courage, and inspiration for your own journey.

Caroline Rochon

As an International Speaker, Trainer, Success Coach, Professional Organizer, and Premiere Partner for Appreciation at Work™, Caroline's journey since she left the corporate world in 2007 has been filled with accomplishments, including the *Self-Employed Entrepreneur of the Year Award* in 2010.

Caroline believes in paying it forward by sitting on Executive Committees and Board of Directors of various organizations, such as Big Brothers Big Sisters, and the Heart and Stroke Foundation. She is fluent in both English and French and inspires everyone around her with her authenticity and vitality.

Caroline has joined international speakers on stage in Mexico and at a TEDx™ Conference in India. She is a multifaceted personality as a television and radio columnist, author and speaker.

www.carolinerochon.com

SECTION 1: CHAPTER 1

CLARITY Leads the Way to Success!

by Caroline Rochon

> *"Her CLARITY gave her purpose and her purpose gave her CLARITY." Jonathan Stroud*

The morning of July 2nd, 2011—after I woke up from being drugged and raped—something became crystal clear to me. I made the most powerful binding agreement with myself. It was a pact that I felt with every fiber of my being: I made a choice, that from that moment on, I would live every day on a path of love and joy.

Why so much clarity after going through a traumatic ordeal? In hindsight, I can attribute it to a habit—the habit and the knowledge that when I am clear about what I want to be, do, or have, it leads the way to success. I knew that if I wanted to have a positive outcome after what had happened, I needed to be clear on how I wanted to live in the aftermath of that experience. The path of fear and anger was not how I wanted to live my life. My daily mantra became unequivocally, and still is: "Today I choose to live on a path of love and joy."

That is not to say that I don't feel fear, anger, anxiety, resentment, guilt, despair, and unworthiness at times. But when those feelings show up, and I recognize them, I immediately ask myself: "What can I do to move myself back onto the path of love and joy?" Sometimes it takes me a week, sometimes an hour, and sometimes only a minute before I'm successful.

Being clear is both a habit and a belief. I am certain that if you practice clarity, you, too, can obtain the success you want. But like Abraham Hicks says: "It does not matter what I do. I cannot tell you what to do to get clarity. You need to feel your clarity! And that I can only teach through the clarity of my own example." So let me share with you why, in the midst of one of the most difficult experiences of my life, it was so easy to be clear.

Fearlessness or CLARITY?

Most people attribute my success to me being fearless, but I know that clarity is the key to my success. In my experience, every time I got clear about what my heart truly and genuinely wanted, I received it. I emphasize what the heart wants because there is a big difference between what the heart and the mind desire. Do you remember having moments of clarity and what developed from that?

I left my pension to follow my passion!

I started my business part-time in September 2005. Then in January 2007, I got clear I was sending a double message to the universe. I was keeping my job because I didn't have faith in my capabilities to succeed in my business. It didn't take long before I resigned from my project management position with the government. I like to say *I left my pension to follow my passion.*

I soon made a vision board of where I wanted my business to be...no holding back: I included images of being on television, doing radio, becoming a spokesperson for a national product, and giving presentations. I dreamed big. My motto: "Dream big or go home!" So I did. In my head, all these things would happen over an extended period of time. One thing was even clearer: I wanted to become the French household name for decluttering and organizing.

That type of clarity is not something you know, it's something you feel. It is an epiphany. It is an inspired feeling versus a thought. I carried that feeling within me without thinking about it. I had no expectations of how this insight would happen; I just allowed it to be without any resistance.

CLARITY makes vision boards come true

TV – Radio – Spokesperson
CLARITY = Excitement and Opportunities

Within two years of having intense clarity and making a vision board, all these successes appeared in my life.

I get excited now when the phone rings because so many times on the other end is someone wanting to offer me what I want most. Here are a few significant examples:

A TV producer called and asked me to audition to be the organizing expert for a popular French television show. I thought I would go for the experience of auditioning, thinking it would serve me later on. Through applying a few success principles, I got the job and signed a year-long contract.

Later that year, I was sitting in the car with my then husband and, out of the blue, clear as day and without a thought, I said: "We are switching radio stations." As I pressed the button to change the dial from an English 'rock' channel to a French talk radio station, I cried out, "because I'll be a guest expert on *that* station!" The following week, a radio host telephoned me and offered me a position as a regular guest on their show.

Another time, I was preparing labels for an organizing client when I ran out of supplies. The store only had their brand name and not the ones I usually buy from Avery®. When I got home and to the task at hand, I started cursing these labels because they just weren't up to standard. A few days later, a public relations firm contacted me and said their client was interested in me becoming their French spokesperson. I was surprised, their client was Avery®!

This clarity of wanting to be the French name for organizing and decluttering created opportunities that went beyond what I thought possible. First, it produced an ongoing excitement that I nurtured through my daily actions. The ripple effect produced by this clarity and the positions as spokesperson, TV personality, and radio personality was gratifying since it allowed me to share my message and empower a larger French audience.

I did not want to become a statistic

Releasing 75 pounds
CLARITY = Focus

After suffering numerous miscarriages, depression and dealing with life issues, I attempted and failed several times to lose my excess weight. It wasn't until I gained clarity on *why*

I wanted to lose the extra pounds that I released them and have kept them off ever since. I was truly enjoying the life I was creating as an entrepreneur. One thing was clear: my body would not be able to sustain me with the life I was aligning. It was evident to me that I wanted to be responsible for my happiness, but I also wanted to be responsible for my health and not rely on pills or the government to maintain me in life. In my family, there is a list of people with heart problems and diabetes.

It was clear to me that I did *not* want to become a statistic. For a full year, I ate only proteins and vegetables...no sugar, no dairy products, no alcohol, no bread, none of the "good stuff." I started drinking water, plenty of it! Within a year, 75 pounds came off! The bonus I did not expect was most of my health issues (such as 14 days of headaches per month, bad PMS, acid reflux, and fatigue) all disappeared as well! This clarity gave me so much focus. It empowered me to say 'no' to the bad food and unhealthy choices and say 'yes' to health, energy, stamina, glowing skin, and vitality.

Book
CLARITY = Manifested Desires

During a conversation with an author acquaintance, she said she was under a writing deadline and her home did not provide the proper setting for her. I shared that I was writing a book on tips to get organized, but recently my intuition was telling me that I should write my personal story about the journey from struggling with clutter to becoming a professional organizer. She said it was a great idea. The next day, I called to invite her to spend four days in my camper trailer by the water, where we would have the peace and quiet to write. I wrote 80 percent of my book, and she met her deadline.

The following month, she called requesting me to print my manuscript and cancel my plans for Thursday because I was going to meet her editor in Montreal. I had not worked on the book since the trip. At that time, I had heaved my words onto paper without proofreading it. This was going to be a disaster, but I said the universe is opening a door for me and I would learn from this experience. A month later, I got the news: they wanted me to finish my book because they wanted to publish it. The title in French translates to *Me and My Clutter – Confessions and Secrets of a Professional Organizer.*

This clarity allowed me to manifest my desire of being a published author. Most of all, it fulfilled my desire to help people by sharing my story and inspiring them into action.

Wisdom to create CLARITY

Training Program and Path of Love and Joy
CLARITY = Healing and Inner Peace

During a year-long training program, I gained clarity on my personal and professional life. Initially, my husband and I had envisioned our future with children. Unfortunately, that vision of a family never happened for us, and I was clear I wanted to leave a legacy if not through children, then to all the people I would influence through my work. After some heartfelt talks, we re-evaluated our life as a couple, and we both realized we were on divergent paths. We loved and cared enough about each other to separate, eventually divorce, but continue to be friends.

Three weeks later on July 1st, my first time out as a single woman, the outcome of the evening was not anything I could have imagined. I was drugged and raped. After I had regained consciousness, clarity came to me immediately, where I made my vow that from that moment on, I would choose to live every day on a path of love and joy.

That clarity paved the way to healing beautifully and brought me deep inner peace. I needed to focus on myself, so I took a year-long sabbatical to learn how to take care of myself and, most importantly, to love myself. It was clear that I needed to tend to my emotional well-being if I wanted to pursue working in the personal development world.

Dreaming big with my bucket list

TEDx Talk, India, and Better Life Day, Mexico
CLARITY = Expansion

At the beginning of my year of self-love, I made a bucket list that was more aligned with who I wanted to be. Just like my vision board, I allowed myself to dream big and not censor myself. I put on that list all the countries I wanted to visit, famous people with whom I wanted to have dinner, experiences I wanted to have, etc.

At that point in my life, I was getting clarity that I wanted to transition my career to be a speaker and trainer.

Seven months after creating my wish list, I received an email which made me say, "W*ow!* This clarity thing does work!" Puja Gupta, a wonderful lady I had met during my training with Jack Canfield, invited me and other friends to be speakers at a TEDx™ event that was being held in her hometown of Chennai, India. On my bucket list, I had "Visit India", "Be a TEDx™ Speaker", and "become an international speaker!" Going on this trip, I checked off three things in one opportunity!

A year later, I was invited to speak at an entrepreneurial event in Monterrey, Mexico, where I was among a list of top international speakers.

This clarity allowed me to expand my reach and my comfort zone since I spoke on *The Power to Choose* when facing a difficult situation (the choices I made after the rape). It expanded my career, my vision, my growth, my network, and, most of all, this clarity expanded my self-esteem.

We are looking for a partner

5 Languages of Appreciation
CLARITY = Stability

Dr. Gary Chapman's book *The 5 Love Languages* allowed me understand myself better, as well as shed light on some of my relationships. I told my client this concept needs to be incorporated into businesses. When I returned home, I noticed on their website the word 'Appreciation.' When I clicked on it, I landed on *The 5 Languages of Appreciation in the Workplace* website. I couldn't believe it: this concept already exists. The book of the same name by Dr. Chapman and Dr. White truly reflects what I was sharing with my client.

I signed up for their newsletter, and a week later I received an email from the VP of Dr. White saying they had noticed I was a speaker and trainer. They were looking for partners and wondered if I would be interested in speaking with them. What you don't realize is that a month prior to this email, I had gained clarity in my business. I wanted to enter the corporate world through the heart—focusing on human beings not 'employees.' My partnership with Appreciation at Work™ allows me to put forth my vision!

> *"More important than the quest for certainty is the quest for CLARITY."* Francois Gautier

This clarity is giving me stability in my collaborations, in my finances, in my focus, and in my long-term plans.

Since my sabbatical year, I have learned the art of letting go and living through inspired actions. The 'how' and the 'when' do not belong to us. We don't need a plan or clarity on *how* to get what we want. I believe we are our own worst enemies when we want to control everything and require certainty in everything. Is there an area in your life where you would gain benefit if you chose to let go?

I know that practicing clarity throughout the years has brought me excitement, pleasure, opportunities, focus, manifested desires, healing, inner peace, expansion, stability, and, ultimately, success. I am on a constant quest for clarity. I know it is a combination of habit and strong belief. This is so ingrained in me that, even when something goes wrong, it just allows me to empower myself with what I want. It fuels my inner being because it is not something that I *decide;* it is something that I *feel.* When I am clear, nothing stands in the way of my personal or professional success! Clarity allows me to be congruent with my heart, my mind, and my focus through my inspired actions.

I hope my stories inspired you to let go of certainty and to embrace clarity. Invest in knowing what you are passionate about; in knowing your values and what you stand for; in knowing the *why* behind what you do and what you want.

Let CLARITY exude from every fiber of your being and let CLARITY lead the way to your personal and professional success!

Success Strategies

1. Create a *Vision Board* by making a collage of words and pictures that increase your excitement and energy.

2. Check in with your *passions* and *values* on a regular basis. *The Passion Test* from Janet and Chris Atwood is a great resource.

3. Write your *Bucket List*. Note all the things you want to be, do, or have—without analyzing the details of how or when.

4. *Meditate* and *visualize* a minimum of twice per day. I recommend doing this first thing in the morning and last thing before going to bed—even if it's only three minutes. Allow yourself to breathe and center yourself, and then feel what you desire as if it has already manifested.

5. *Honor your true authentic self.* Embrace who you are and live your life, not what other people expect you to be or do.

6. *Connect* with how you want to feel every day. Start noticing the difference in how you feel between your inspired actions and your *To Do* list.

Notes

Lourdes Carmona Gutiérrez

Lourdes was born in Elche, Alicante-Spain. Despite being from a family with no background in aviation, from an early age she wanted to become a pilot. She is now a believer in self, a flight instructor, a mother, and an airline pilot.

She's the creator of *Listos para Despegue* ('Ready for Take-off' in English) which lifts others up and helps them live the life of their dreams, eliminate their limiting beliefs, and find their true nature and life purpose.

www.listosparadespegue.com

SECTION 1: CHAPTER 2

Believe to Achieve

by Lourdes Carmona Gutiérrez

> *"I stand for freedom of expression–doing what you believe in and going after your dreams."* Madonna

The day of my lucky 13th birthday, I received a phone call letting me know that a letter I had submitted was the winner of a contest. My parents and I were invited to travel to the U.S. to visit Disney World® in Orlando for ten days in a Magic Kingdom® Resort! At that time, my hobby was to send letters to any nationwide contest. This hobby gave me many benefits, including this trip. Since that contest, I have won over $12,000 USD in prizes.

I was excited to visit America for the first time, but I did not have the faintest idea I was about to discover my passion for flying.

I had the time of my life on my first transoceanic flight from Madrid to New York. After landing in JFK, I saw a female Captain using a public telephone in the main terminal building. I will never forget the power this image had on me. She was an apparition: the sunlight reflected on her; she was beautiful and stylish. I could hear a soft voice in my head repeating "that is you in a few years; she is your reference." That is what I call a miracle!

Being aware of your inner voice is like finding a lighthouse in the middle of a storm whilst sailing the ocean at night. *Finding your own success images is a key factor to gain confidence in yourself,* and then to *believe* is much easier. Your subconscious mind knows there is another version of yourself—successful and capable of anything.

After that trip, I started researching how to become a Pilot. It required me to change my life 180 degrees in order to be aligned with my dream, but I was ready to make it happen. I found my first roadblock in the suggestion that I apply to the Army. The selection process was challenging: I was 40 pounds overweight and a Literature student...but I had to be fit and study Science.

Overcoming Obstacles

When I was a freshman student in High School, my internal self-talk was louder than ever. How could I possibly make it? I was not interested in losing a few pounds before starting the beach season, it was about being *fit* and ready for the Army and, of course, about studying Math and Physics. I *believed* I *could make it.* I was not too late for my plan; I had plenty of time for accomplishing a realistic goal. People asked me, "What is your diet? Are you taking any medication?" It was amazing to feel lighter and full of energy. My 'medicine' was my own satisfaction, and my diet plan was far from boring. I started an exercise plan of aerobic classes 3 days per week and lifting weights. My breakthrough goal was strong enough to keep me motivated.

I had three years to achieve my goals before finishing High School and I accepted my strategic plan with motivation and drive. One day after class, my dad called me to his office:

"Lourdes, I know you are making great progress with your Science classes; I just want to make sure you are doing the right thing." "Yes, dad, I am," I replied. "Sweetie, have you considered you suffer from motion sickness? I know you want to become a Pilot, but it might not be your best choice."

Yes, that was the story of my life. I always remember travelling and feeling dizzy—anywhere, by any mode of transportation. That was a *huge* roadblock. Guess what? I was so focused on the *what* that I completely forgot about the *how*.

Giving My Auto-Pilot Signals for Success

The way I overcame this obstacle was by visualizing that I was one step away from my dream! The motion sickness disappeared as if by the wave of a magic wand, through the power of my visualization of flying high—wearing my Pilot uniform and watching the world from above the crowds. I felt free to dream big and became the director of my wildest dream. And it worked for me!

More challenges surfaced along the way, many of which I brought on myself. However, when I faced reality from a different point of view, I became much stronger than before and then felt able to make my dream happen.

I am curious about the way we respond to road blocks in our path. We are trained to react in the same way over and over.

Our 'Autopilot' system knows how to process our 'software signals,' but what about when your dream is not aligned with your program? Yes, go for updates. Be willing to adapt. *Believe in yourself.*

My teachers used to tell me the importance of being proficient in English if I wanted to become a Pilot, so I went back to the U.S. as an exchange student. It was my second trip to America. I was a senior in Northwestern High School in Albion, PA, and had the time of my life. I still miss my American dad's pancakes and his pocket pizza. After my graduation, English was no longer a challenge to the pursuit of my dream of flying.

It was not easy—I was only 17 years old and it was my first time away from home by myself. It helped me to remember and focus on *why* I was there and to have the best experience possible, living with joy during the time spent with my new friends and my American family—my beloved Siviks. The most helpful learning I gained from this experience came from my own behavior—adjusting to a new culture takes an open mind. After this process, I had new resources and ideas to apply to my life on a daily basis. I was more mature and ready to rule my world. I have been dreaming *big* my whole life. *I believed in me.*

Living My Passion

After graduating high school in Pennsylvania, I came back to Spain in June 1996 and joined an International Flight School. I graduated at the top of my class, but before finishing my studies, the school principal called me to his office to offer me a Flight Instructor job. I agreed and started working for them. I discovered my life purpose: teaching and helping others to reach their highest vision. I was more than a Flight Instructor, I was a motivator. I learned to listen to my students' needs and fears. I played a key role during their training and I felt responsible for their progress. My top priority was to help them *believe in their dream.*

During my time as a Flight Instructor, I lived with passion. For three years, I built up more than 1,800 hours of training and gave more than 2,000 hours of lectures. I was on 'Cloud Nine' every single day. Then I applied to a top Spanish airline and got hired. I have been flying jets for more than 10 years now. Yes, *me!* Me—a skinny girl, far from overweight and able to lift up a 36-ton jet airplane with just one finger!

Everything has a process. I want you to know that you will succeed—just watch your steps along the way and enjoy. Keep in mind your final destination, carry the vision with you whatever it takes, and surround yourself with people who lift you up. Be your best admirer, respect your own body, rest enough every day, and love yourself—*believe in you!*

Keep your eye on the prize, because sometimes along the journey there are silent moments when it seems nothing is going on and everything moves too slowly. If you start feeling like a fish swimming upstream, that is a good sign—keep following your master plan. It means your baby steps are moving you forward along your path.

Unshakeable Faith

Flying with confidence through a cloud is a great example of the unshakeable faith I have in my cockpit instruments. I relate those instruments to my master plan: whenever I am not able to see the *how* during the process in my daily life, my master plan guides me. When flying through clouds (which are a form of liquid droplets or crystals made of water suspended in the atmosphere), sensory illusions may appear, giving a false horizon line for level flight. This sensory phenomenon can be dangerous for pilots—the flight crew is aware of it and strictly follows the flight instruments. When setting goals, use your master plan as your flight instrument—check it continuously as you go through the process.

Being ready for success is about commitment and taking responsibility to face your reality and do what it takes to get closer to your goal. To *Believe* makes things possible.

My personal story has helped me to gain self-confidence. Having a wild dream was not enough; setting goals and moving forward played a big role in my process. When looking back at my teenage years, I only had thoughts of courage and determination with unshakeable faith—step by step knowing I was going to make it someday, somehow.

Some of my classmates thought I would never make it. *But I believed in me.* I took small steps to overcome my personal obstacles and conquer my world. Going to the gym, I felt weird, thinking I had to lose 40 pounds. But I felt amazing when I changed my jean size every two months, going from size 14 to a petite 4! I walked outside my comfort zone: I didn't know if I would be able to pass all my Science subjects, not to mention graduate in a foreign language in a different country. If I had the chance to chat with myself as a teenager, I would hug her hard and let her know how proud I felt of her accomplishments.

Now, it is you reading my story. Let me tell you: *you are a winner already.* Be ready to explore and live your wildest dreams—there are no wrong decisions. They all help you grow with every step of the way—you become wiser and your experience is determined by your actions. Make decisions like a winner—just *Believe.*

"Adventure is worthwhile in itself."
Amelia Earhart

Success Strategies

1. Keep your *destination* in mind. Find an image of success, like the female Pilot I saw when I went to Disney World®.

2. Have *unshakeable faith.* Never give up on your dreams, regardless of perceived roadblocks along the way.

3. Use the power of *visualization* to put your mind on auto-pilot towards your dreams. It takes 30 days for your auto-pilot to kick in and create new habits that will lead you to success.

4. Divide your dream into *smaller goals.* Tackle them one at a time to reach your dream.

5. Never stop *believing* in yourself!

Estelle Nuka

Estelle is a fellow of the Association of Chartered Certified Accountants, and has over 25 years' experience in finance and auditing. She is married, with two children and one grandchild.

Estelle is a member of the Board of Directors for several institutions in Malawi, including NBS Bank, Malawi Energy Regulatory Authority, Pakachere, Francis Palau Hospital, and United General Insurance.

She established EWN Consulting & Training where she combines her experience and skills gained from the Canfield Training Group to coach and train clients in success principles and financial management.

Estelle is passionate about women and the less privileged, especially disabled children.

www.ewnconsultants.com

SECTION 1: CHAPTER 3

Perseverance - The Fuel of Success

by Estelle Nuka

> *"For every failure, there is an alternative course of action. You just have to find it. When you come to a road block, take a detour." Mary Kay Ash, Founder Mary Kay Cosmetics*

On 28th December 1993, I decided to write a letter to my mum. I had hardly finished writing the first paragraph when I received a message that my mum had passed on. It was crushing. She had not been sick, so it didn't make sense to me. I didn't believe the news, but I still decided to go to the village, all the while thinking that it could, instead, be my father that had passed on. He had been sick with Parkinson's Disease for some time.

When I arrived home, there were *two* bodies in the house: my mother's *and* my father's. And the twist in the tale is that it was my father who had killed my mum before killing himself. It was like going through some horrible dream. And I was six months pregnant.

I couldn't handle it. I fainted; literally, I fainted.

Becoming a Professional Accountant

When I finished high school in 1984, I applied to study Business Studies at The Polytechnic, a constituent college of the University of Malawi. My choice to study in this area was based on a beautiful office with the inscription 'Chief Accountant' engraved on the door at my cousin's workplace. I had said to myself then, "One day I should occupy that office." I knew very little about accounting, let alone what a professionally qualified accountant was.

I first heard about The Association of Chartered Certified Accountants (ACCA) while at the Polytechnic. I didn't understand a whit about it until my roommate, Joanna, enlightened me. (Joanna had attended one of the elite high schools in Malawi, hence her knowledge.) She hinted that qualified accountants earn more than mere accountants.

After I graduated, I joined Price Waterhouse—beginning an accounting career that was to span 26 years. Price Waterhouse paid for my training, and allowed me one day a week to attend classes, at the Malawi College of Accountancy, to train as a professional accountant.

During my training, there were two incidents that almost made me quit. The first was when I received the wrath of my manager. I did not provide a conclusion on a job that I had done—I felt I needed more time. (This was against a background where the time allowed for the job had been reduced.) The manager reported me to the managing partner. The partner then asked me to provide the conclusion, otherwise he was not going to sign my training contract (which I needed to be certified). Despite the risk of not having a training contract, I maintained my position, because I strongly *believed* it.

The second incident was when I was sent to an Outward Bound course in Chimanimani, Zimbabwe, for three weeks. Apart from being very challenging, it was also dangerous. I had to walk in some areas near the Mozambique border, which had land mines.

Persevering While Raising Children

In 1990 I got married, and in 1991, I had my first child. With family life, school, and work, I found myself entangled in a web of activities. One thing had to suffer, and that was work. My job required that I should often work outside town, sometimes even outside the country. I decided to resign and join an organization that would not require me to travel as much.

The professional training for accountants in Malawi had three levels. I completed level two of my studies soon after I had joined my new organization and now needed to go to college on a full-time basis to complete the third, and final, level. If I were still working for Price Waterhouse, I would be certain they would sponsor me to go full time, however, with a new employer, this was not possible. This meant I had to choose between continuing with work and tendering a resignation to go to school at no pay at all. One question troubled me a lot: who on earth was going to pay for my college expenses?

I reminded myself that my goal was to become a professionally qualified accountant. To achieve that, there was no other route but full-time training. So, still staring the financial challenges in the face, I made a decision to pursue my dream...and I was now expecting my second child.

Life was tough—tough in the honest sense of the word. On many occasions, I felt like quitting. I had no means to prepare for my baby, who was due three months before the date of the exams. I would need to prepare and sit for the exams, and I had no choice but to think about who would take care of my baby those three months.

With all the financial challenges at hand, and considering the fact that the baby would be very young, I felt that my mother was the best, and only, person to give my baby the best of care...but she was living some 750 km away. I had to make the request through a letter, which was the only sure means of communication between us at that time.

The letter was never sent. Mom died the day I was writing it. From all reports, my mother tried to stop my father from taking his life and the gun went off by accident. Then he turned the gun on himself. I was faced with another tough decision: do I continue with school knowing there would be no one to take care of my baby? With a lot of pain and a very heavy heart, I decided to persevere and continue with my training. My baby was born on 31st March 1994. With no one to care for my new baby, I had to quit my training and miss three months of school.

Qualifying Against all Odds

> *"Persistence is probably the single-most common quality of high achievers. They simply refuse to give up. The longer you hang in there, the greater the chance that something will happen in your favour."*
> *Jack Canfield, The Success Principles™*

The challenges I faced after I quit my first job, as well as the trauma I went through due to the sudden death of my parents, were enough to make me quit on many fronts. Pain had been as true as life to me, but I chose to persevere and continue with my goal of becoming a professional accountant. I studied for the rest of the course on my own. I passed the exams and five years later was granted the honor of being a fellow of the ACCA.

Seven Long Years of Waiting

While I met a lot of hurdles to qualify as a professional accountant, setting up my consulting and training firm took much longer than I had expected. In 2006, I was privileged to attend a three-week course in Public Finance Management at Duke University in the USA. It was a class of 40 participants from all over the world. Towards the end of the course, one of the lecturers asked a question that made me jittery. "How many of you have savings equal to eight months of your salary?" None of us raised our hand. He stated that, at the time, it was taking approximately eight months to get another job after losing one. Therefore, to have peace of mind, I needed that much savings in an account.

I did not have eight months savings and I wasn't sure I could manage when my money was sufficient only for my everyday needs. I decided to buy a book on personal finance, hoping it could come to my aid. The title of the book I read was **Smart Women Finish Rich** by David Bach. Later I also read **The Power of Focus** by Jack Canfield. Having experienced positive results within a short time after reading those books, I felt the need to share what I had gathered with others. Despite my desire to share immediately, I felt it was necessary to get approval from the authors. I tried to contact the two authors, but nothing materialized; I am not sure my communication reached them.

There were times when I felt like giving up. But the more I continued to apply the lessons I had learned, the more I felt the urge to share. Seven years later, I saw Jack Canfield on Facebook® and immediately 'Liked®' his page. The next day, I saw a post inviting up to 100 people from around the world to attend the *Train The Trainer* program and become trainers in *The Success Principles*™. I thought I was dreaming. That was too fast. I could not believe it. I had been trying for seven years and here was an opportunity within my reach. I decided to go for it.

A Passion without Resources

When I checked the details of the program, I noted that I qualified straight away. But there was one problem: the fee was impossible for me. The training was to be held in the U.S. and would require me to travel three times within one year.

Having resigned from my job six months earlier, I was not earning anything. So where could I find the money for tuition and three round-trip air tickets from Malawi in southern Africa to the USA? How about hotel accommodations and upkeep? Despite my doubts, I went ahead and submitted my application. I was interviewed and accepted into the program. But where was the money going to come from? I was told there were no scholarships. The only consideration available was a 10% discount.

I could not afford the remaining 90% tuition and all the related expenses without draining my small savings drastically. I therefore decided that I could not attend. However, that did not mean I had given up on my goal! I enquired if they had a home study version. I was informed that it was "in the pipeline." I had no choice but to ask that I be considered for the home study once it was available.

Although I still do not know what happened, I got an email from Jack Canfield welcoming me to the same course that I thought I could not afford. I had not confirmed my attendance, so I was puzzled. However, Jack was the person I had been looking to connect with for over seven years. I decided to reply and explain my predicament.

Jack is one of the kindest and most generous people I have ever met in my life. Having read my email, he asked the coordinator to "see what could be done" to enable me to attend the training. The rest is history. In the midst of perseverance, I was given flexible terms to make my training possible.

As part of my training, I needed to do a one-day workshop and send feedback to the trainers. I have never been as prepared for a presentation as well as I was for this workshop. Unfortunately, two days before presentation day, I could not fully open my mouth. *I was told that I had experienced a minor stroke.* I needed my voice for my training! I was prescribed one week of bed rest—but that would mean cancelling the workshop. While I rested for the required week, I still went ahead with the workshop. It was not easy, but having prayed over it, I decided to face the challenge.

I have now established my own consulting and training firm, and I am happily sharing knowledge that I have always wanted to share.

Conclusion

Do not give up on your dream, no matter how long it takes. Sometimes in life we are able to achieve our goals without waiting that long, and almost without shedding a bead of sweat or a tear. That is fine, but, in most cases, achieving the goals that we are most passionate about requires time and perseverance. We need to hang in there, eyes wide open, hands on the steering wheel, and success will surely come—no matter how long it takes.

I endured a lot of challenges to qualify as a Chartered Accountant. As a result of persevering through all those challenges, I earned the qualification that has enabled me to work in various senior positions. It took me seven years to achieve my goal of sharing and training. It would have been easier to tire midway and quit because of the frustrations. But I hung in there, despite everything and everyone telling me to throw in the towel. Giving up is easier when faced with a challenge because there is no effort required in giving up. However, the pain and regret of *not* doing it may have more serious repercussions than the temporary solace one experiences after giving up.

So, unless *all* the feedback is telling you to quit, do not quit—press on. A Malawian proverb says, "A trapped struggling boar only squealed when the hunter's rope around his neck was about to snap." The wild pig here was on the verge of setting itself free; if it had endured a little longer, it would have been free. The answer is perseverance—help may be just around the corner at the time you think of giving up.

As Jack Canfield says, "There is no such thing as failure, only delayed results." Make sure you stand up more times than you fall down until you achieve that goal.

Success Strategies

1. Where there is a *will*, there is a *way*. Refuse to give up, no matter the circumstances. Find creative solutions to overcome obstacles.

2. Stuff happens along the way. When you least expect it, life will throw you an obstacle. It may slow you down, but *don't let it stop you*.

3. When someone tells you N*o*, do not take it at face value. I always *believed* I could do it, and never took N*o* for an answer.

4. In life, there are many challenges and there is always a *choice*. You can either allow these challenges to derail, or even stop your progress, or choose to move on. The choice you make determines the quality and magnitude of success awaiting you at the other end.

5. No matter how difficult and daunting the situation, if you choose to *persevere*, you will surely come out victorious!

Lori Harder

Lori is a leading expert in the fields of fitness, transformational work, mindfulness, and self-love. As a successful entrepreneur, network marketing professional, author, cover model, and three-time fitness world champion, she offers a carefully curated set of practical tools to promote sustainable health, spiritual well-being, and financial freedom.

Through her books, unique coaching methods, and programs, she has helped countless people connect with their souls, transform their bodies, empower their minds, gain financial independence, and fall in love with themselves and their lives.

www.loriharder.com

SECTION 1: CHAPTER 4

Discipline is the Key to Success

by Lori Harder

> *"You have to know you're worth the gift of self-discipline.*
> *You have to invest in the learning curve of loving*
> *yourself through keeping your own promises."*
> *Lori Harder*

I stepped up to the diving board. I was ready. I walked to the edge of the board and took my form. I heard yelling off in the distance. Could it be cheering? It was coming from the corner of the pool where my crush and his friends were floating around. I was trying desperately to overcome my self-consciousness and poor body image. Not wanting to miss out on any flattering words—I yelled back, "What did you say?"

"Don't jump in the pool, you whale!" It happened so fast, like a punch in the gut. "There won't be any water left for us," he taunted. I had no idea that words could grow hands and reach down into your body, tear out your heart, and smash it on the ground like it was nothing at all. One day at the pool and my life was changed forever.

That day on the diving board was the first time I felt pain. Since then I've learned that, without feeling pain, I would have been too comfortable to create the changes that I needed to in order to feel confident in myself. It took me a few years, but this pain became my motivation, and my motivation fueled my discipline.

Creating a new habit was not a discipline problem for me. The problem was that I had no reason to want to change, no reason to leave my comfort zone. That is, until my reason became a pain so unbearable that I was reminded of that childhood pain—pain that I never wanted to experience again. Not only did I want to have self-confidence, but I wanted to teach it to other people who felt like that little eight-year-old girl at the pool. I wanted to feel better and to help others learn how to take control of their own lives and feel confident.

In my adolescence, I had habits that supported short-term gratification. I would feel bad and eat something to make me feel good. I would feel bad and watch something on TV to make me forget. Habits like these continued to feed my anxiety and fuel my issues with my body and my self-esteem. The fixes were quick, but then I was left feeling terrible. I knew that something had to shift.

Exercise—my way out

Exercising was new to me, so I had to start small. I would walk, rollerblade, or dance for 10 minutes—any activity that would spiral my body and brain into wanting *more* activity. It wasn't long before I became obsessed with fitness magazines, health books, and my older sister's VHS workouts (ah, the '80s).

Moving meant feeling better. The challenge was that my family was not active and I was not in any school activities, so finding ways to stay moving was up to me. I was responsible for keeping my life in motion, and it was hard work.

Making this change took time and a lot of daily coaxing. "Just take the first step," I remember telling myself. "Just move and you will feel better." Anytime I negotiated myself out of an exercise routine, I would force myself to recall how I felt when I didn't exercise. *No, thank you, to feeling all that pain again.*

Even though I became far more active and much healthier, I continued my battle with food. Dieting was all I had ever known. This was what my mom and sister had been doing my whole life. Since we were all overweight, we were all either on a diet or back to our old bad habits—there was no middle ground; we were all or nothing. Spending family time together was either cooking in the kitchen, eating around the table, going out to dinner, shopping trips with snacks, or movie nights with pizzas...or it was a strict diet that no one could stick to for very long. We lived on both ends of the spectrum: diet and restriction = no fun; food and indulgence = mega fun. Neither was healthy.

Eventually, I realized that the accomplishment of completing an exercise routine felt so much better than any short-term reward. Exercise was my way of earning happiness for each day, because the only thing that worked for me was a disciplined fitness regimen—the discipline that came with the fitness regimen gave me a sense of control.

Looking back, I know that not finding a new and healthy replacement for family fun time was a huge reason that we could not stick to our diets. Now, with fitness, I was the one who had a say in my outcome. Discipline was freedom from pain. The act of restricting my indulgences—those old habits and quick fixes—opened a whole different set of options and opportunities I had never known existed.

Stepping out–and falling down

When I was 18, I moved out on my own, and it broke my mother's heart. I deeply loved my family and had nothing but a warm upbringing, but I also knew that I had to remove myself from their habits and religious restrictions in order to figure out who I was and what I was capable of becoming.

I had no clue what I would do or where I was going, and that's pretty much how the next few years on my own progressed. I was a gypsy: I job-hopped from waitressing to sales to becoming a make-up artist. In between job-hopping, I was bar-hopping, and along with that came friend-hopping. I was doing what people do when they are out to 'find themselves.'

What I found was a lot of trouble. Some situations were serious, others were life-threatening, but none was enough to wake me up from my victim coma. I had convinced myself that I was stuck—that this was my fate. Every action I took was in an effort to numb out my feelings. I was anxious and my heart was ready to riot. Here I was again, living like the little girl at the pool—feeding my fears and wallowing in my lack of self-confidence. I was lost and my soul was calling for help.

A disciplined fitness practice had led me in the right direction before, and once again it proved to be reliable. One activity or workout at a time, just like before. When I was moving, I felt good. When I felt good, I was happy. When I was happy, I could hear what my soul was trying to tell me. "Clean up your life!" Okay, that's a start.

Trading Bad Habits for Good Habits

I had a fitness routine, I read the magazines, and I reaped the rewards. This time it even led me to my husband. Yes, we met at the gym (which is a great spot if you want to meet like-minded people). Fitness kept me out of trouble and away from late nights, because I didn't want to skip a day at the gym—a day of feeling good. Fitness encouraged me to make better choices, because I didn't want to eat food that made me tired or wouldn't help my results. It kept me motivated and interested in creating something positive for myself. I had something that I could fill my time with that was productive, healthy, and made me proud.

These new habits enhanced everything I was doing. Even my relationships improved because I respected myself more and started to like who I was. I began to feel like I had an identity. Fitness was no longer something I had to think about. It was just something I did no matter what. It was my new habit. It was a discipline that created a solid foundation of health, clarity, and strength to build on.

I was falling in love with how I felt having the discipline of health and fitness in my life. I wanted to bring this into other areas of my life, but I was struggling trying to figure out how.

It's all or nothing, right?

That's the mentality I had when I stepped up to become a personal trainer. I opened up a small gym and made the choice to begin competing in professional fitness competitions. I had this crazy dream that one day I could be on the cover of the same magazine from which I had once gleaned my own motivation. Perhaps I could become that same inspiration for someone else, and gracing the cover was where I needed to start. All I wanted was my story to give them proof that no matter what your background, you could make anything happen. But my self-talk was out of control: "You're not good enough for this—or smart enough. Who is going to listen to you? You're a fraud."

There I was, existing on only one end of the spectrum or the other—again.

My motivation for fitness had always been the fit and inspiring women in magazines, so it was clear that one thing I did do naturally was observe what successful people did. I wanted to make money, to have my own business, to help others, so rather than only watch the highlight reel of my mentors, I looked further into their struggles and starts. Ten minutes at a time.

There I found a common interest—a common discipline. They were into self-development. While I was—and most of them were—a lover of all things fitness, I realized that at 26, although I'd read a lot, I'd not read a thing about self-development or business. Just like I did with fitness, I started out with 10 minutes of disciplined reading every morning.

If I missed a morning read, I didn't beat myself up. I just set the goal again for the next day, and the more I did it—holding myself to 10 simple minutes—the more I wanted to create even more time to read. Any time that I started to negotiate myself out of it, I would remember why I was doing it and how good learning made me feel. This habit initiated earlier bed times so I could fit in even more reading time. Eventually, I no longer had to think about making myself read, because—like fitness—reading became a habit that was born from a disciplined practice that started with just 10 minutes.

Learning self-love

The next few years were spent pursuing the edge of my comfort zone and taking leaps, all with the help of my disciplined reading practice. This introduced me to a woman with a concept: Gabrielle Bernstein says, "I am willing to see things differently. I am willing to see love." When I read these words they totally rocked my world. It was a life changer. I had no clue that loving yourself (what?!?) is necessary in order to become successful. In fact, I had believed the inverse: the harder on myself I was, the better and stronger I would become. I mean, who doesn't respond well to being told you're a piece of crap ten thousand times a day? Okay, fair enough. Fear can push you at times, but when you find yourself beating your head against the wall, take that as a clear sign that what you are doing is no longer working.

Insanity

I might have been reading inspirational and informational material to my heart's content, but I was the definition of insanity. I was doing the same thing over and over and expecting a different result. Anytime I felt like I was detouring, I became very hard on myself and set up restrictions. However, I was getting the opposite effect of what I wanted. Rather than feel motivated, I wanted to rebel against my own restrictions.

In the effort to start my own business, I had become fairly successful—with clients and a nice place to work out—but I was hitting a wall. And I definitely was not having any fun. Having muscled myself into this version of success, I was stuck, tired, and knew I could not keep up with the battle in my head. I didn't love my life, so how would I ever help others love their own?

How could I teach them to create a life of their dreams when I felt stuck in a rat race? I had the confidence and the knowledge, but I was in desperate need of some loving guidance about what to do with it all. I had learned so much—about being able to retrain a healthy body and mind, and create a money blueprint—that I was becoming highly aware that I needed to focus on loving who I was in the present. I no longer needed titles, accomplishments, or accolades to get noticed or bring me love.

Self-awareness

Gabrielle Bernstein's concept of choosing love over fear was an answer to my prayers. The only thing that brings me true happiness is being grateful for who I am and what I have. I had to learn how to express my authentic self so I could share my love with the world. Self-awareness became my new practice—no more going through days on autopilot allowing life to happen. I was becoming the creator of my life through my thoughts. I was now an active participant.

The more disciplined I became in catching my negative thoughts, the quicker I could correct them and the better I felt. Every small shift and ritual that I had added, one at time, was helping me to create different outcomes. It became exciting to see what my mind was capable of. I exercised. I read more books.

The deeper I dug, the more I found out that science had already proved what I was now figuring out on my own: we are not stuck with the brain with which we are born. Nor are we stuck with the stories and willpower we learn in our youth. Instead—through disciplined practices—we can change the way we think, feel, and perceive life, which, in turn, alters our outcomes and reality. I learned that we actually have the power to create *willpower*.

My power is willpower

> *"Be just as proud of the things you say 'no' to as the things you say 'yes' to."* Robin Scharma

Willpower lives in a part of the brain called the prefrontal cortex. It operates like a muscle: the more you flex it, the stronger it gets. But there's a catch: we only have a set amount of willpower in a given day. Many of us waste it on decisions and choices that are not important, because we don't have a plan and we are not clear about what we want. We spend the day dwelling on low energy thoughts and trying to convince ourselves to do things we don't want to do—and by the end of each day we are worn out and have nothing left.

So, what if I could create more willpower?

The good news is that the prefrontal cortex can actually grow by getting exercise, sleep, and meditation. When you don't get the sleep you require, the prefrontal cortex does not function properly...then we don't create an adequate amount of our natural appetite suppressant and we keep ourselves from making better choices throughout the day. In a nut shell: when we don't sleep and we don't exercise, our willpower actually decreases.

Who's got the time?

For many of us, adding more sleep and a fitness routine to our daily lives means adding time and—since we can't add hours to our day—what we *can* do is eliminate things in our day to create time to do the things we love. I *found my new discipline.* In order to create a life I love, full of rituals I love, I had to be able to say No to the things that were distracting me away from saying Yes to the life I wanted. I was saying Yes to fitness and living healthy. I was saying Yes to reading and learning about my career choices. I was saying Yes to getting truthful with my authentic self. But there was a whole lot I couldn't say No to. I was a people pleaser, as I imagine many of you are, too. You may not think you fall into this category, but I don't think your idea of fun is disappointing people. Disappointing people was my fear.

A disciplined No practice changed my life. Starting to say No was the toughest part, but once I did, I noticed how good it felt to clear space in my life. Don Miguel Ruiz writes in **The Four Agreements** "to be impeccable with your word." This meant it was time for me to really honor my *Yes's* and *No's*. Sometimes we use *Yes* as a temporary form of happiness. We can say *Yes* to make someone feel good and break that promise later. This was causing me more anxiety than saying No because I had to think about this and deal with breaking that word down the road.

Eventually, I learned to say No in a polite way. We can all practice this in small ways. Maybe you need more down time just to recharge—start saying No to going out with friends during the week. Maybe you are overwhelmed—say No to helping with a neighborhood bake sale or helping a friend move.

Here's the truth—you know you're doing it right when not everyone likes you or your choices. For a lot of your friends or family, saying No may mean you are not as readily available or accessible for them. However, this could also mean that you're no longer someone's scapegoat, sounding board, or doormat.

Discipline is freedom. When you implement just a little bit every day, over time you can create everything you desire in your life and you will begin to feel the deep satisfaction of accomplishment and the ownership over your choices.

Success Strategies

①   Release the *All-or-Nothing* approach to life. Ten minutes of disciplined action each day can lead to much more.

②   You can create more *willpower* by getting the appropriate amount of sleep each night, 20 minutes of exercise, and/or practicing meditation each day.

③   In order to carve out time for the things you want to do, you may need to *start saying No* to other things. As Jack Canfield says, "Say *No* to the good, to say *Yes* to the great."

④   Use the *discipline* muscle in small ways every day to make it grow.

⑤   *Learn to love yourself*. Keep your promises to yourself.

Susan Treadgold

Susan is a coach, speaker, and transformational trainer. In addition to one-on-one coaching, she runs a series of 'Masterclasses' designed to help women thrive both personally and professionally. She also runs an annual *De-stress and Assess* Retreat at her home in Southern France. She is passionate about helping people to live big lives and create more of what they want by increasing their 'Energy Engagement.'

Susan has worked with organisations such as Kings College London, Royal Bank of Canada, Investec, Jefferies, Barclays Bank, BroadMinded, Women in Business, Women in Banking & Finance, London Women's Forum, American Business Women's Group, and TeachFirst. She lives in London, England, with her husband and two cheeky children.

www.tedlondon.com

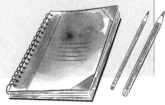

SECTION 1: CHAPTER 5

Engage your Energy

by Susan Treadgold

> *"Nobody but you is responsible for your life. You are responsible for your life. What is your life? What is all life? What is every flower, every rock, every tree? Energy. And you're responsible for the energy you create for yourself, and you're responsible for the energy that you bring to others."* Oprah Winfrey

MIND Energy

*A*t 5:50 a.m. my alarm went off. I could hear the low hum of the jetliners making their way over sleepy London as they started their descent into Heathrow. I immediately slapped the snooze button and, like a brainwashed zombie, settled in for my daily dose of negative self-talk.

"I am *so* tired. I hate my job. My boss is such a jerk. My co-workers are *all* annoying. And my clients are *so* rude. I don't want to go to work," I whined silently.

"What could my excuse be for staying home again today? Boiler bust? Burst pipe? Food poisoning? Grandmother died (again!)?" On and on I let my mind swirl down the familiar negativity vortex, resisting any earlier resolve to get out of bed on time.

BZZZZZZZZZZZ alarm again. 'Snooze' swiftly slapped and torture talk resumed. Following the third alarm and failing inspiration for any credible truancy alibi, I finally hauled my sorry carcass out of bed and got into the shower. Under the pressure of hot water, my mind chatter expanded into full blown Technicolor™ visualisations of all the misery and horror that awaited me in the office.

When I finally got to work (arriving slightly late and a bit hassled as usual), no prizes for guessing what kind of day I had. My boss was a jerk. My co-workers did annoy me and my clients were rude. Everywhere I looked there was something I could (and did) complain about. A self-fulfilling prophecy perhaps? At any rate, the steady drip of negative thoughts I was thinking and the vivid images I was visualizing in my mind had now morphed into a major leak in my personal energy. I was feeling drained and verging on burn out. Something had to be done (enter dramatic music).

> *"The energy of the mind is the essence of life."* Aristotle

Like being tossed a lifesaver, a series of synchronistic events followed: being seated next to a life coach at a dinner party, landing a copy of *The Success Principles*™ by Jack Canfield, and spotting a synopsis of how Viktor Frankl trained his mind to survive a Nazi concentration camp during WWII. What a novel seed of an idea they simultaneously planted! Actually taking responsibility for my own happiness and consciously choosing my thoughts? Really? I mean really?! Well, it was worth a shot. As Benjamin Franklin famously said, "the definition of insanity is doing the same thing over and over again and expecting a different outcome."

The next morning started with some different choices. There was no more snooze button. As soon as my alarm sounded, I jumped out of bed and shouted (in my best Dolly Parton accent), "I'm wide awake and I LOVE my job," nearly giving my husband a heart attack. Before my self-talk could interject, I switched on 'I Like Big Butts and I Cannot Lie' and did my best, big booty dance (eat your heart out Kim Kardashian)! My shell-shocked husband burst out laughing at the absurdity of my 5:50 a.m. disco and for the first time in over a year, I got an energetic boost from some early morning laughter endorphins.

But old habits die hard. My morning torture talk did not surrender graciously. As I stepped under the shower, a little voice—quiet yet confident—whispered, "But you're not really wide awake—it's 5:55 a.m. For goodness' sake, it's still night time. And you don't really love your job. I mean, how could you, with the people you work with?!" Undeterred, I shouted it down again, insisting, "I'm wide awake and I love my job."

When I arrived at work (on time and with a deliberate smile on my face), I immediately entered into a Negativity Detox pact with the poor woman who sat next to me on the trading floor. No complaining, blaming, gossiping, or whining for an entire week, or a coin would have to be paid into the charity mug on my desk. After the initial rapid fire 'ding, ding, ding' din of clinking coins subsided, we started to get the hang of it. As infectious as our negativity had been, it was a pleasure to find out that our positivity was also equally contagious. At the end of the week, we decided it had been a pretty good week and that we'd continue with the negativity ban for another week.

And then a funny thing started to happen. I started to notice that my boss wasn't actually a jerk (at least not all of the time), not all of my co-workers were annoying, and my clients were pretty polite for the most part. My energy started to surge, my client rankings started to go up over the following weeks and, lo and behold, three months later I was offered a promotion to a job I much preferred. Go figure!

> *Change your mind and you can change your life.*

You have the power to choose your thoughts—the pictures you make in your head—and to seek those things which bring you joy. You are in control; no one else can do that for you. Needless worry, picturing the worst possible outcomes, and focusing on the negative will only cause energy leaks. Positive affirmations, thoughts of gratitude, and picturing the best outcomes are some of the antidotes. The energy you get from the quality of thoughts you choose will create your experience of life. For example, what would your experience of life be like if you were to choose to love (the action verb not the noun) what you do, love where you do it, love who you do it with, and who you do it for?

CONNECTION Energy

> *"Use each interaction to be the best, most powerful version of yourself." Marianne Williamson*

Word had it that my boss was in town. Great—as a manager of a new department that was growing quickly, I always had something for him to sign when he was in town.

I quickly grabbed my folder and walked across the trading floor towards his office. Outside it, I paused and peered through the glass walls to see if he looked busy. He wasn't meeting with anyone and he wasn't on the phone. He was merely looking at his computer screen—perfect time to catch him! I gave a quick knock, popped my head in, and said, "Is now a good time? I just have a quick question."

Without looking up from his computer screen, he replied with a slightly annoyed tone, "Go on then." Sadly, what I had not learned, was that how I chose to communicate with him impacted him energetically. He was an introvert (along with about half of the world's population) and was energised by spending precious 'thinking time' alone. So the meeting was already off to a bad start with my energy-sapping interruption of his thoughts. Feeling a bit miffed that I was not getting the face-to-face interaction that energised me as an extrovert, I reluctantly continued, "This is the X situation. What do you think?" This clearly annoyed him further (introverts don't like to be put on the spot; they need to 'think' about it first) so his sharp, rapid-fire response was, "I don't know what I think. What do *you* think?"

Disappointed at his lack of interaction and brainstorming (another pet hate of introverts) I replied "I was planning to do Y." "Sounds good to me," was his reply, indicating the conversation was over. I walked, shoulders sagging, back to my desk and implemented what I had suggested...and then two days later I got an email (the preferred form of communication of introverts) saying "I've been thinking...I think you should do Z not Y." Then I'd proceed to waste my time and energy, often damaging my credibility as well, undoing the course of action I had already pursued. It will come as no surprise that he was not at the top of my list of favorite people (the feeling was mutual, I'm sure).

Only after the benefit of coaching and understanding the energetic differences between introverts and extroverts was I able to flex my behaviour. Remember, you can't change other people; you only have control over your own actions. Only by making different choices might you influence their likely responses.

Later, instead of knocking on his door without an appointment, I sent him an email (his preferred communication format) saying when I'd like to meet, a précis of the problem, and my proposed solution. Sounds obvious, huh? When I next arrived at his office, he immediately looked up from his computer and said, "Hey, come in, take a seat. I've had a think about the situation and I like your idea X...and you might consider doing Y as well." Well, knock me over with a feather! I was utterly gobsmacked by the sudden face-to-face interaction and his willingness to engage, which I had craved from him for so long. After I left, the course of action we had agreed upon stuck. By accommodating his preferred communication style, I positively impacted his energy and mood. Bringing out the best in him meant I no longer had to waste my time, energy and credibility undoing work I had actioned once he had 'time to think.' With this better CONNECTION energy (surprise, surprise) our relationship also improved.

Armed with this new energetic awareness, I changed how my team meetings were run as well. The agenda was now typed up and distributed to all the night before. This advance notice enabled me to get the best from the less forthcoming introverts who now had a chance to 'think it through,' as well as more considered responses from the extroverts who had previously been prone to 'thinking aloud' their semi-formed ideas to the group. Everyone was participating now. More and better ideas and a happier and more motivated team were the results. Again, a small change in the way I chose to interact with others had a positive, energetic ripple effect.

This powerful source of energy, which you get from the ways in which you choose to interact and communicate with others, is what I call 'CONNECTION' energy. Bringing the best out of people is a skill that is universally useful—be it the way you appreciate, listen, or provide feedback. The quality of your relationships is the biggest clue as to whether you are an energy angel or energy vampire! Better customer service, loving relationships, happy family members, cheerful and productive co-workers, and loyal clients are all symptomatic of good CONNECTION energy. The better you know yourself, the better equipped you are to be a positive influence with positive energy—and that energy will be returned to you.

INPUT Energy

"To keep the body in good health is a duty...otherwise we shall not be able to keep our mind strong and clear." Buddha

I was on the London Underground one day when I saw a teenage mother encouraging her obese, exhausted looking toddler to suck down some Coke® in a McDonald's® cup. I was outraged by her ignorance and wanted to grab the young woman and yell, "What are you doing?" As I sat there silently judging her, I had an epiphany. I was really no different. I was looking after myself exactly as she was looking after her toddler—and I didn't even have the excuse of ignorance. I was overfed and undernourished. When I was not eating at my desk while glued to my computer screen, my travel schedule meant many meals out with too much sugar and processed food. Surviving on five to six hours sleep per night, I struggled to nod off at night and then again to wake in the morning. Coffee and caffeinated drinks were my crutches to get through the day. I was tired and wired.

My body had been giving me pretty serious feedback for a couple of years, but I had failed to acknowledge the heavy hints. Infertility, frequent need for antibiotics, excess weight, dehydration, poor digestion, inflammation in the body, and overall exhaustion were my symptoms. Pretty obvious clues, right?

Picture your body as a pot and your energy as the water. If you have a full pot of water you are able to cook up all sorts of wonderful things in your life. The possibilities are limitless. Allow half of that water (ENERGY) to leak out and your options become limited. Fail to heed the warnings when you are nearly on empty and you can burn out and cease to function.

What I have seen, from past personal experience and the many busy people I have coached, is that you've got to carefully manage your INPUTS. The quality and quantity of the air, food, water, sleep, and supplements you put in your body form the foundation for performing at the top of your game. Common sense, right? But diseases such as cancer and diabetes are rising globally. It seems uncommon sense is required to really create INPUT success habits. Time and time again, I see intelligent, high performing people with great focus and mental strength (MIND energy) and great people skills (CONNECTION energy) run into trouble as inadequate INPUTS such as a poor diet and lack of sleep eventually catch up. If you don't look after yourself, you will simply limit your quality of life and what you can achieve.

Energy is the Key to Success

The one common denominator in lasting success in virtually anything is energy. To create a life of power, passion, and purpose, you need to engage with your energy—become 'energy aware.' Assess where your energy comes from and where your energy leaks are, then put in place (and persist with) energy rituals (cue new habits) that will plug up the leaks and enable you to live an extraordinary life.

> *"Energy and persistence conquer all things."*
> Benjamin Franklin

In my model of Energy Engagement™, I show how your vitality comes from proactively engaging with your six main energy sources: MIND, CONNECTION, and INPUT which I've just covered, plus SPACE (the energy that comes from the objects and environments you choose to surround yourself with), PAUSE (the energy we get when we unplug, tune out, slow down, and get still) and MOVE (the energy derived from the shapes we give our body—from body language to exercise).

The more energy you have, the more results you're able to create: in your relationships, in your career, even in your finances. So spend some time now analysing where your energy comes from and where it goes. Which single change could you make that would have the biggest overall impact on your energy? Do you need to 'train your brain' to focus on the positive, work on or eliminate a tricky relationship...or simply get some more sleep?

Start now, creating some easy energy rituals to plug up the leaks and then add more as your energy grows. For ideas, join my free energy challenge at *www.21DayNegativityDetox.com*, then watch how your extraordinary life unfolds!

Success Strategies

1. The one common denominator in lasting success in virtually anything is *Energy.*

2. You are responsible for the energy you *create for yourself.*

3. Be aware of the energy you *bring to others.*

4. Choose *gratitude and love* (the action verb, not the noun) over lack and fear.

5. *Be Energy Aware.* Know where your energy comes from, where it goes, and how to maximise it.

6. *Carefully choose* the thoughts and images you create in your mind.

7. Proactively engage your six main energy sources: MIND, CONNECTION, INPUT, SPACE, PAUSE, and MOVE. You never really understand something until you apply it.

8. Reassess your INPUT energy inventory (air, food, water, sleep, and supplements) regularly.

9. *Create and persist* with new energy rituals to break through to sustainable success.

Notes

Trisha Jacobson

Trisha is passionately committed to helping people break through fear, overcome blocks, and heed intuitive whispers and heart's wisdom along the path to self-discovery.

She is an intuitive and compassionate teacher who engages her readers, audiences and clients. Trisha shares conscious, subconscious, and heart-centered tools to raise self-esteem, connect with passion and purpose, and develop goals, action, and accountability plans that lead to happiness, success, and fulfillment.

Visit her website to learn more about Trisha's results-oriented services, books, and her Pathways to Success Youth Team.

www.trishajacobson.com

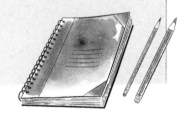

SECTION 1: CHAPTER 6

Authenticity - Discovering Your Inner Magic

by Trisha Jacobson

> *"Authenticity is a collection of choices that we have to make every day. It's about the choice to show up and be real. The choice to be honest. The choice to let our true selves be seen."* Brene Brown

*I*n August 2011, in the midst of a difficult break-up and some major financial hardship, I had a profound metaphysical experience that rocked my world, challenged my core beliefs, and gave me a whole new perspective on my life and the challenges I was facing. The experience forced me to confide in a close friend and share the messy details of my circumstances which, up until then, I had kept to myself. It was also necessary for me to reach out to some non-traditional resources for support I needed to fully integrate the metaphysical experience. My story isn't something I would normally have chosen to share over dinner with my family or in the office by the water cooler. I kept my truth well hidden back then.

A few days after the event, I woke up from a sound sleep at 3:35 a.m. to a voice telling me that the final chapter had been revealed. It was time for me to write my story. "Now," the voice said. "Start writing now."

Three weeks later, clearly led by divine inspiration, I finished the first draft of my manuscript. It sat on my computer for two months before I let anyone read it. It was my story; the same story that looked perfect to so many from the outside looking in, but was raw and ugly on the inside. It told of my pain and struggles through addiction, divorce, financial hardship, career transition, a geographical move, failed relationships... and ultimately through healing to awareness, forgiveness, joy, light, and love. The book played a major role in moving me closer to my authentic self, but I had no intention of sharing it with anyone. That seemed unnecessary...and very scary.

The voice nudged me once again. "Your story needs to be shared. It will touch many. It will give them hope for their future and help them find the tools and concepts they need to explore on their own journey. And you will be healed in the process."

I can still remember the day I hit send and released the final manuscript to the publisher. I felt completely vulnerable. Fear rippled through my body as I imagined being judged and scrutinized for what I had written. It was too late. I had just shared my story with the world...honestly, openly, and authentically.

A week later the book was released. I loved the feedback I got, and still get, from my readers. They thank me for being so transparent. They share bits and pieces of their own journey and tell me how my book helped them take their next step. There were some who questioned the legitimacy of the wild abstract experience that prompted me to write the book in the first place. But what stands out most was, and still is, the connection I feel to myself and others by taking the risk and sharing my journey authentically.

My story is powerful...messy, yet powerful...just like yours. *The key is to embrace the messiness, accept ourselves just as we are and take the risk to connect with others openly and honestly so we can heal.* As we heal, our message is allowed to unfold and ultimately have an impact.

In her book, **Daring Greatly,** Brene Brown reminds us that "our story can be hard, but not nearly as difficult as spending our lives running from it. Embracing our vulnerabilities is risky, but not nearly as dangerous as giving up on love, belonging, and joy. Only when we are brave enough to explore the darkness will we discover the infinite power of our light."

At some point we are faced with some of the bigger questions: "Who am I? What do I value? What am I passionate about? What is my purpose? What am I here to accomplish?"

Is this all there is to life?

As our stories unfold, some of us choose to follow an already prescribed path laid out for us by our parents, mentors, culture, profession, or society. For many of us, the bigger questions come later in life—after our education, career, marriage, family, major purchases; that time when we look around and wonder if this is all there is to life. For some, the questions are prompted after a life-changing event, such as divorce, job loss, illness, death, or financial difficulty. Some might look back over the course of their lives to see patterns and cycles that held them back from ever finding true meaning or happiness in life.

At some point, we will be challenged to go within, beyond the noise of the day-to-day lives we have created and deep down to the core of who we really are, to the place where we connect to our authentic source.

So how do we do that? Where and when do we even begin?

It's simple. So simple that there is no way anyone can say this is too much to add to an already full plate. Let's begin right now.

Face it. There are days or even some periods in our lives when we are in survival mode, just doing our best to take care of our basic physiological and safety needs. I encourage you to try some of these strategies anyway.

ACTION: Notice, just simply notice, what makes your heart beat happy.

You know the sensation that rushes over you in the instant when you are happy or experiencing joy? Notice where you are, who you're with, what you're doing, what you're seeing when you look outside yourself. What is happening around you, or what are you thinking when that feeling happens?

That 'sensation' is the result of a dose of serotonin—the feel-good, well-being chemical that releases in your brain. It's the same chemical that brings on good feelings when you are immersed in an exciting project, or during yoga, meditation, and orgasm.

The good news is that there are many simple ways to increase your serotonin levels. It's a little different for each of us, but it takes hardly any time to get an extra dose of this feel-good chemical throughout our day, as long as we know what works for us.

I have my students compile a *25 Things That Bring You Joy List*. Then I have them fold it up, laminate it or put it on their electronic devices and carry it with them wherever they go. Whenever they are stressed, frustrated, and angry, or simply need a dose of serotonin, I tell them to take out their list, pick one thing that brings them joy, and do it. Then, do another until they feel more fully present in the moment, thus connecting to their authentic selves.

ACTION: Go ahead right now. Brainstorm a list of 25 things that bring you joy and make your heart beat happy. Start using it to increase serotonin in your brain, joy in your life, and get more deeply connected to your authentic self.

Keep in mind that this does not need to be complicated. One of my mastermind group members connected me to the work being done by the HeartMath™ Institute saround transforming stress, building resilience, and connecting with authenticity. My youth program was experiencing some significant budget cuts that created a stressful work environment and had me wondering how I was going to pay my bills. As part of our conversation, Tricia gifted me an emWave™, a tool used to practice getting into what the HeartMath™ Institute terms 'coherence.'

She instructed me to place my thumb on the monitor, practice rhythmic breathing while focusing on what I'm grateful for in my life. The result I was looking for was to cause the red indicator light to turn to blue and then to green, which meant I was in coherence. With practice, she instructed, I should be able to maintain coherence for a set period of time a couple of times a day, which would help me better manage my life from a heart-centered space, reduce stress, and increase well-being.

I simply couldn't do it. I got to green for about 30 seconds once or twice, and to blue for a bit longer, but I couldn't maintain it. One day, I lay on my couch determined to relax, breathe, get to green, and maintain it. After yet another unsuccessful attempt, my cat Leah decided to join me. She jumped up onto the couch and settled on my chest. The emWave™ was still in my right hand as Leah nuzzled my left hand with her face, suggesting I pet her. As she began to purr, I felt my heart beat happy. At the same time, the indicator light went from red to blue to green. As I continued to snuggle with Leah the light stayed at green for a solid half hour. Pets really do help reduce my stress and make me happy.

I no longer use my emWave™. Nor do I need to follow any special meditation ritual, take another personal development class, or read another self help book. I now know that a five-minute cat snuggle does wonders for my being...as does a spoonful of Ben & Jerry's® Chocolate Therapy ice cream, my first sip of coffee over sunrise, a heart hug from a coworker, clean sheets, hand warmers in my pockets after a day of skiing, and that special moisturizer I use after the shower. It truly is the simple things that make my heart beat happy, remind me of what's really important to me, and help me to live authentically.

Like many women in my generation, I was raised with the idea that taking care of myself first was selfish. Today, I redefine what my Mom called 'selfish' to be 'self-care.' Self-care has become the foundation of my life, my work, my relationships, my goals, my hopes, and my dreams. A great resource for helping us embrace the concept and connect with the idea of self-care is a book called ***The Art of Doing Nothing*** by Veronique Vienne. I've also discovered that when I'm in that place of joy—fully present in the moment—ideas, insights, and inspiration flow through my consciousness like some sort of magic.

Passion and Purpose

The next step in the journey towards living authentically is to examine passion and purpose. What would life be like if all our decisions were made with the goal to increase passion in our lives and bring us closer to our unique reason for being on the planet? My teacher and mentor, Jack Canfield, introduced me to *The Passion Test* by Janet and Chris Atwood, along with a number of ways to explore life purpose in his book, *The Success Principles*™. I highly recommend you check out both.

Today, all my life decisions are based on my *Passion Test* results and the life purpose I've created for myself. If it's not a "heck, yes!" I simply don't do it. When I find myself in the midst of something that is not in line with my passion and my authentic self, I give myself permission to step back and evaluate. I am in the process of doing that right now.

I recently took on an interim position as the director of the ski school at which I've been teaching for the past fifteen winters. I am passionate about skiing and love sharing my passion with others. However, I've quickly discovered that my new management position doesn't allow me to teach and train as much as I'd like to and has me spending most of my time doing paperwork and managing schedules. My boss just approached me about my plans for next season. As this season winds down, it's time for me to step back, evaluate and see if I can turn it into a better experience for next year.

The clearer I am about what I need and want, the more authentic action I take. I am in the process of developing a cohesive management team that is passionate about what they do and willing to serve from a place of connection. I am discovering that the authenticity I bring to the table makes them more willing to allow their core genius to come through and help me create the joyful life I am looking for.

The coolest thing I've discovered is that there is always someone out there who is totally passionate about the things I am not. They help me live authentically and I help them do the same.

We are creating our reality all the time. The only choice we have is whether we are creating it consciously with intention according to our values and desires or unconsciously by default. Creating consciously with intention and coming from a place of authenticity is truly where our power lies.

Creating a Magical Life

The real magic is that the simple joys lead to the bigger things that ultimately lead us to a deeper connection with our authentic selves. For example, my connection with animals plays a role in where I live and who I live with. My passion for skiing influences my winter teaching and coaching schedules.

Why do we wait to discover who we really are or to answer the bigger life questions? What is the real source of our fear that prevents us from embracing vulnerability, taking risks, and sharing who we are with ourselves, each other, and our world authentically?

There is no longer a need to wait until later on in life or until major life events occur to take your journey to authenticity. You can start today, right now, in this moment.

What will make your heart beat happy
in this moment? Go do that.

Success Strategies

① Discover what makes your heart beat *happy!*

② Practice being fully present in those *joyful moments.*

③ Expand your self-awareness by exploring *passion* and *purpose.*

④ Get *support* to break through fear that may be blocking you.

⑤ Share your *authentic self* with others.

⑥ Live with authentic *integrity* to make your life, your work, and your relationships a "Heck, yes!"

Section 2

Striving for Success

SECTION 2: INTRODUCTION

*W*hat separates the wheat from the chaff, successful people from the masses? What makes one person strive for more and work harder, while others are content to sit on the couch or take it easy? The answer is *Ambition:* that striving, reaching, stretching oneself to be the best you can be.

Striving for Success contains the stories of ambitious women from around the world who found a way around obstacles to succeed. Lawyer *Sharon Cahir* strived for, and found, success in spite of a recession that rocked Ireland. *Michelle Garnier-Chedotal* of the United Arab Emirates is the master of reinvention, constantly striving for self-improvement and teaching others tools to improve their own lives. Executive Chef *Beth Gardner* shares how staying open to possibilities allowed success to flow into her life, while Dr. *Mayra Llado* designed her ideal life as a Cosmetic Dentist in Puerto Rico. England's *Amanda Brown* stares down one of our greatest fears: Feedback. Amanda shares how she went from shrinking from feedback to seeking it out in order to better herself. Entrepreneur *Jean Ann Reuter* inspires us with her story of decades of persistence, one of the meta-themes you'll see emerging from the stories in this book.

These women are as different as night and day, yet their ambition to get ahead in life—their striving for achievement—is a beacon to guide us on our own paths to success.

Sharon Cahir

Sharon is a charismatic Irish lawyer, award-winning entrepreneur, and successful business woman with a reputation as a strategic thinker and intuitive connector of people, information, and business enterprises.

As a captivating speaker and transformational trainer, Sharon engages her audiences with business insights and storytelling. She inspires women to play at their highest level in entrepreneurialism, leadership, and life. *Soft Power—Strong Results* and *The Connectors Compass* are two of the energising and empowering talks and workshops delivered by Sharon internationally to high-performing women.

Sharon lives in Ireland with her husband and three energetic and amazing sons.

www.sharoncahir.com
Twitter: @sharoncahir

SECTION 2: CHAPTER 1

The Art and Abundance of Connection

by Sharon Cahir

> *"We are like islands in the sea, separate on the surface but connected in the deep."* William James

In the Beginning

I was excited. I had knocked three times, as was usual, and waited intently to hear her footsteps. Once she opened the door, I knew there was a long afternoon of laughing and chatting and what many would call 'light work' ahead of me.

Three times a week, I would spend my after-school hours with my grandmother and today was a special day. I was going to help her and her trusted neighbor, May Glynn, prepare for a church event that evening. My grandmother, you see, was a key character in my young life. I spent a lot of time in her presence and in her home as it was within walking distance of my school and a stone's throw from my parents' workplace. It was convenient childcare but the loving and lasting impact of those after-school days would shape my relationships with others. The value I would place on building the relationships would shape my life, my business, and my success.

Nana or Sisty, as her friends called her, was a religious woman. Her three-storey terraced house was located on a narrow street directly opposite the Catholic Franciscan Church. It was no surprise that her religious life, her social life, her connections, and her friendships revolved around the church. On this particular day, she and her neighboring friend had the responsibility of making the sandwiches for a church gathering. I began to regard their gatherings as a very important event in their connected lives. The chat, the laughter, and the shared volunteerism gave them a purpose and a contribution to their community.

> *"The most important single ingredient in the formulae of success is knowing how to get along with people."*
> Theodore Roosevelt

The joy my grandmother and her friends derived simply from being with each other, sharing the project, and celebrating their contribution together, was blindingly obvious to me. What influenced me was the laughing and learning together and their desire to give back to their community. The more time I spent with her, the more I observed how happy and content she was being connected to a tribe of like-minded people.

Through her example, Nana instilled in me the need to be connected to others in order to succeed in the world. Brene Brown said in her book, *Daring Greatly,* "We are all hard wired to connect with others; it's what gives purpose and meaning to our lives."

An Emerging Leader

I spent my teenage years as a student in a boarding school and, as the only girl in my family, I relished the idea of living in a school of young girls, having great adventures and midnight feasts.

The day I arrived at boarding school my excitement was over the top. However, my dad, a lawyer by profession and inclination, wasn't convinced that dropping his daughter off at the front door of a large imposing structure in a small country town called Thurles was an inspired decision! Despite his reservations, it was the perfect place to build friendships, connect with my peers, and develop collaborative sharing of ideas. Learning to bridge different perspectives and points of view was the beginning of my journey as a transformational leader.

I spent four years living in that school as my home, growing up with friends and experiencing life as a teenager—first as a student and then as a young woman hungry for life and all the promise it held. Regardless of any trials and tribulations, I always had the support of my friends, my teachers, and my mentors. Our togetherness sustained and nurtured us. Four years of life with my peers gave me the connections, confidence, and ability to grow into the best version of myself.

The conflict I most vividly remember connected us all in a story we still recount to this day. Two nights before our final exams, we all assembled for bed excitedly. On this night, we did not have to be asked twice to put the lights out. We had planned to celebrate my birthday and our last midnight adventure, each girl taking a turn to stay awake once the lights went out. When midnight came, each student in our group rushed excitedly to find the glorious food packages we had hidden from the nuns so we could have our last gastronomic midnight feast. The excitement was palpable, and the whispering and laughter got louder as we uncovered the Black Forest *Gateau* sent by my mother.

The warmth and connection of four years of camaraderie, constant communication, and boarding school culture spilled into the air loud enough to wake Sister Maria. Suddenly, the door pushed open. The unveiled, red-faced, angry nun stood before us and decreed with authority that the feast was over and our sleep-in the next day was cancelled. We would rise at 7:00 a.m. for Mass, followed by a stern speech, study isolation, and a letter to our parents outlining our disobedience. She said that we lacked the responsibility of young leaders. In our hearts, we disagreed—the connection we had as friends and allies supported us through the conflict and confrontation we experienced that weekend.

In both these formative periods of my life, I was aware of the importance of women being my supporters, friends, and confidants. Indeed, this is a theme that has resonated throughout my life. I remain connected to many of the girls I grew up with during that era. The connection we have is unbroken by time and distance. We are joined by invisible threads and shared memories.

Former United States Secretary of State Madeline Albright said, "There is a place in hell for women who don't support other women," and I totally agree. Connecting with positive, like-minded people from a place of integrity is a recipe for abundance not only in financial terms, but it is food for the soul as well.

Who are you connected to? Consider how they support you and connect with you in challenging times.

Islands in Time

From an early stage, I learned that networking has to be more about *connecting* than *collecting* contacts. Connecting means going deeper into the nature of relationships, learning what is important to someone. It's more than superficial conversations and merely working a room collecting business cards.

"The connection economy thrives on abundance: connections create more connections." Seth Godin

Connecting with people and embracing networking opportunities were key motivators when I returned home to lead the family law firm in the late '90s. Less than two decades later, the firm had doubled in size and our awards for professional services and customer excellence adorned our reception area. Constant connection underpinned our growth and success as a business; and the most valuable connections I made during those years were with my team. Working as an engaged unit focused on opportunities, overcoming challenges, and embracing change allowed us to go from good to great.

I had experienced similar success and team connection in my first career as a young hotelier. My general manager was a relatively young, dynamic Irishman who sought to make a real difference in the industry. He reached into the community and connected strongly to ensure his hotel was the establishment of choice. His reliance on his team to deliver international standards of excellence was a heavy burden, but his leadership and passion delivered the clarity and motivation we needed to excel. I remember team meetings that connected us and ignited our passion to deliver with excellence.

We were inspired to be great leaders of our respective teams. Ever since those days and throughout my career, I have aspired to be truly connected to myself as a leader as well as to my team, my customers, and my search for excellence.

True connection in business comes from building a relationship of trust. Without trust, there is no connection—it's like a car without petrol. You can be in it all day long and get nowhere. Networking in the wrong rooms can be soulless and lead you nowhere.

As a constant connector, it was normal for me to be out and about, but as Ireland plunged into recession, the air of negativity sucked out the social oxygen. The media was churning sad story after bad recessionary story into the public domain about businesses closing, rising unemployment, and emigration at an all-time high. The Celtic Tiger's roar had turned to a whimper. Business owners and their employees were struggling on the cold front of despair. I was connecting less—and when I did, I wished I hadn't. The warmth, friendliness, and depth of connection in Ireland as I knew it was gone.

Although I had always enjoyed networking, it now became a negative experience in my life. A black cloud had descended over Ireland and infected every community with negativity. The business community was no different. The air felt heavy and the future seemed loaded with austerity and challenges. I needed to connect with positive like-minded company. Life will always present opportunities to connect, but who and what you connect to makes all the difference. I needed to laugh and learn despite the austerity.

My proximity to an international airport brought the world closer. In early 2011, I boarded a flight to London where I began my career over two and a half decades earlier. If you were a passenger on that flight, you might have seen me smile as I felt I was about to rise above the dark recessionary clouds. I knew that if I wanted different results, I needed to make different decisions. I needed to take massive action and find a supportive forward-thinking peer group.

That year I began reconnecting internationally. I sought out like-minded speakers and thought leaders to hold me accountable for the vision I had for my life going forward. I wanted to become an international speaker and author—to live my life to the fullest and make a difference. Designing the life and business I wanted led me to this amazing group of women change-makers and transformational leaders.

Brene Brown defines connection as the energy that exists between people when they feel seen, heard, and valued. Being connected to the right people at the right time makes all the difference.

What groups do you belong to? Not all connections are uplifting. Respect yourself enough to walk away if needed. Make sure you connect with those who serve you, support you, and make you happy. Remember, courage is the first quality of a warrior, and it takes courage to know when it's time to move on in life and in business.

Internal Connection

> *"I define joy as a sustained sense of well being and internal peace-a connection to what matters."*
> *Oprah Winfrey*

George Bernard Shaw—that cantankerous observer of the human condition—concluded that life wasn't about finding yourself, it was about creating yourself. I've adapted that to mean that you can live life on a conveyor belt, reacting to what's passing by, or you can choose to go back to the drawing board, work on the design, and create what you want your life to be.

As a Lawyer, Coach, and Trainer I regularly work with clients on succession plans and the need to design a successful strategy for transition in life and in business. The economic turbulence has brought us to a new frontier and people are thinking more introspectively about the quality of the lives they want to lead and legacy they want to leave. I have never had a client tell me at retirement or on their death bed that they wished they had worked harder or spent more time at work. What I do hear regularly are regrets about not travelling more, having better relationships, changing direction when opportunities presented themselves, and living a more passionate life. I have prided myself on being close and connected to my clients, but that proximity began to impact me with sadness the more I dealt with individuals and families who felt they missed out. It made me reflect, too.

They say life begins at 40, but as I entered my fourth decade and welcomed the arrival of my third son into the world, the financial earthquake of 2008 began. My dream life as I knew it would never be the same again.

I was now working what felt like 24/7 as a lawyer and entrepreneur. I was a super-mom to my children, super-daughter to my parents, super-wife, super-connected and chief inspirer, nurturer, and influencer to three future leaders! I was (as most women are) a connector, a multi-tasker, and a generous giver of time and energy. As the waves of financial change crashed against the Irish shorelines, I became super-focused to learn lessons from the challenges and changes with which I was now faced.

The global economic platform had totally shifted and so had mine. In February 2010 my husband and I lost a large retail business and a valuable property portfolio. I was now in the midst of a deepening recession and among the many business people who were working much harder for far less. Staff layoffs, cost reductions, and declining sales became the order of the day.

What I began to see was how disconnected I had become from my own life. My focus had become all work and no play.

I had become so busy with connecting outwards to my team, my clients, my family, and my business opportunities, that I discovered the one person I had not connected to in a long time was myself.

Have there been times when you have been surrounded by friends or family and still felt alone? Are you doing what you love or is it time to reassess and redesign?

As the heroine of my own story, redesigning the life I wanted meant that I had to reconnect to myself. I had to rediscover my passions and my purpose, uncover what it was that made me tick and made me a better person. In the last few years, I have redesigned my life to include my love of family, writing and motivational speaking, travel, making new connections, and, most of all, my love of adventure. I had lost connection with my vision for my own life and my 'W*hy.*' I redesigned my days and rituals to include more fun and more of what I wanted out of life. I like to say completing my first skydive in 2014 was a redesign and reconnection to my adventurous side!

Life can have us plugged in all the time. It gets very noisy and sometimes it's necessary to disconnect, to sit still in silence, and to reconnect.

Mother Theresa said, "Be happy in the moment. That's enough. Each moment is all we need, not more." In an age dominated by mobile communication, I believe she might now say, "Be still and connect to yourself as well."

Success Strategies

1. Review your list of female friends and contacts—with whom do you need to *reconnect* and spend time?

2. Review your networking and relationship strategy for business—connect smarter and deeper. Don't just collect cards, collect *connections.*

3. What groups have you outgrown? Are there negative groups or people who don't serve you any longer? From whom do you need to *disconnect?*

4. Reconnect with *yourself.* Commit to a daily routine of disconnecting from your plugged-in world. Learn about mindfulness.

5. Recollect and reconnect to your *passions.* Make a 'joy list' to re-discover what makes you smile and what it is you love to do for *you.*

Michelle Garnier-Chedotal

Michelle is an entrepreneur, motivational speaker, and Accredited Kinesiopractic® Faculty Member, driven by the desire to put her energy and skills to work for organizations and people who have the courage to transform. She is profoundly effective in combining her in-depth knowledge of energy healing as a Professional Kinesiopractor® with her extensive experience in business, leadership, and coaching.

Michelle founded Kinesio Coach, the only Institute of Professional Kinesiology in the Middle East, where she teaches, coaches, and helps people live the life of their dreams. Her unique ability to tap into energy allows her to deliver highly effective strategies and techniques that help achieve organizational, professional, and personal objectives.

www.kinesiocoach.ae

SECTION 2: CHAPTER 2

Self-Created

by Michelle Garnier-Chedotal

> *"Have Courage, Be Kind, and Believe in Magic" said Cinderella's mother to her young daughter just before she died. The little girl was left alone. In her heart, she knew she was blessed and could create her destiny, but could she believe in magic?*

My body is 58 years old today, and as I approach the autumn of my life, I begin to reflect on my experiences —some of which I have enjoyed and some of which I have found extremely challenging.

Six months ago, I proudly opened Kinesio Coach, the only Institute of Professional Kinesiopractic® in the Middle East. On my way to the office yesterday, I read on a huge billboard— "What are you waking up to?"

As I was pondering that question, a line of the Lord's Prayer popped into my head—"Give us this day our daily bread." I smiled as I knew instantly that it was not about 'wheat and water' but rather about another breath of life, another gift of life itself so I could grow my soul one more day. The only question I had for myself then, was, "Am I fully awake, and in love with life itself? "

Growing Up

I grew up in an environment filled with fear and pain, sexually abused from a young age, not knowing who to trust, ashamed and wanting to *fit in*. My mother, Jeanne Besneux, was born in a small village in Normandy and married her sweetheart from junior school, Raymond Garnier, my father. She had six children and three jobs, because my father was a drunken, violent husband. He was a welder; she was a housekeeper. He had lost himself. She believed he could recover.

When I think about it, my heart is still smiling as I remember my mother's enormous courage and the pride she put in her work, and yet my heart is still crying deeply for what she was seeking then. She lived a life of struggle, pain, broken bones, and humiliation. She finally asked for a divorce when my brother and I were 14 and, on that day, I took a deep breath. My father never changed and died of liver disease seven years later. I knew that their hearts were still connected despite never recovering from anger, fear, melancholy, weaknesses, and constant promises ending in failures.

Moving Out of My World

At 16 years old, I sold the only thing that belonged to me— my saxophone—to buy a one-way ticket to the United Kingdom to take an *au pair* job, learn a second language, and move out of my world. I could no longer witness the pain on my mother's face as she struggled to earn a small income and put both my twin brother and me through school, feed us, and pay the never-ending bills. Learning English was a good first option for me.

My twin brother left school at the same time to join the Navy. I knew my mother's dreams would be shattered, as she lived only to see both of us through college. I left home terrified and alone.

After England, Italy was my next destination. I was hungry for sunshine, romance, and beauty; I fell in love with Rome and Tonino. He loved me, but I could not recognize feelings of love within myself as yet. I left the *au pair* job I had and headed back home.

I worked night shifts in the emergency department in our local hospital, bathing the sick, preparing the dead for their families and, in between, washing the never-ending dirty floors on my hands and knees, with black soap and water. This gave my ego a massive slap in the face and deeply opened my heart! Looking back, I am so grateful today for that experience.

I was determined to earn enough money to go to Paris and attend a two-year tourism school. I wanted to travel more, take my mother with me, and discover a world she could not even imagine. I had just turned 19 when I took the train for the capital. I was lucky enough to quickly find a part-time job helping two kids with their homework in the evenings; my compensation was a small, cramped attic room and an evening meal.

My mother died one year later—she went to bed and never woke up. She was 63 years old and I knew she had prayed for God to take her away in a warm blanket of peace. Her prayers were heard. She died in her sleep, alone, in full surrender. I was devastated, angry, abandoned and alone, and yet somehow, somewhere in my heart, I felt relieved for her.

Looking back, I am grateful that despite her passing, I was able to move on, one step at a time, trusting life itself once I could positively reframe my 'not so good' history. I had to learn to have a strong smile that would never be shattered by the trials of my circumstances.

What to Do Next?

I had no money; I was 19 years old, spoke English and Italian, but had no other skills, except determination, courage, and a desire not to stay in my small town where the only jobs available were working at the post office, the local factory, or the supermarket.

I was clueless about what to do next.

> *"Have Courage, Be Kind, and Believe in Magic"* said Cinderella's mother before she died!

When I saw the movie, I felt that these were the words my mother had instilled in me throughout her life. There was so much resonance in those words for me. My mother had courage, she was kind and gave all she had, but I am still not sure if she ever gave herself permission to believe in magic. I *had to create that part!* I knew that if I could hold on to that truth with indomitable will, I *could materialize anything I wanted.* I also knew that once I said, "I will" then I would never give in.

And yet, strong will was not my issue! Life helped me to develop it through circumstances. "I can change; I have the will to change; I will change my life" was my mantra. What I did not have was a *dream.* I did not know what, where, or how my life was to be. I started meditating, prayed to God, and allowed myself to surrender to His wisdom.

Changing My Life

When I got my first tourism job on my 21st birthday—as a reservation clerk for a chain of hotels—I jumped for joy. *I could finally stand up and walk tall.* I had asked for it in prayer and in a big loud voice. I learned that day to ask, and when you ask with your heart open, it is granted.

Hard work, long hours of dedication, willingness to achieve and to be accepted for who I was, took me over the years to the position of Regional Director of Marketing for the most prestigious French five-star hotel chain. I travelled the world, stayed in the best hotels, and loved life.

I have never been competitive, but when the company launched a sales challenge, I jumped in! I was in heaven! Not just because I won the contest as the only woman competing, but also because the prize was one week in Mahe, in the Seychelles Islands, where I met the man who was to become my husband.

Although that might sound like a fairy tale, it soon became a nightmare. I discovered, on the last day as I was packing my suitcase to go back home, that he was married. I believe in fairy tales but one thing I am sure about, is that I do not want to be the ugly one in them. My whole life has been lived by "always desire that which is good, that which is noble, that which is pure, then you can never fail to attract anything you want!" And that ugly ending did not match my belief.

I met him again three years later, and that is when he asked me to go to Dubai where he was based. Putting things into perspective, we are talking 30 years ago and my friends thought I was insane—frankly, I could not agree more. I had to look at the map to even find where Dubai was. I had made stopovers there on my business trips to Australia, but I did not know what to expect. I believed that if God had put that man twice on my path, I had to listen.

Dubai

With my qualifications and background, it was not difficult to find a job and I was promoted within a few months to a full executive position at the most prestigious property in Dubai, the InterContinental Hotel. The city was small then and everything, literally everything, was happening at the hotel. I had 10 amazing years. I got married, and had my first child. When I was pregnant with my son, I was called by HH Sheikh Mohammed bin Rashid Al Maktoum's Engineering Office, and asked to come and work at the Dubai Creek Golf & Yacht Club, a new landmark for the country.

My mission was to put Dubai on the map as a 'golf destination' in support of the Sheikhdom's goal to grow tourism. The job might have looked prestigious, but I learned that success comes with knowing what you want, having the skills and tools, and doing what you know by breaking a sweat! I took nine days off after delivering my son and went back to work full-time. It was hard work, long hours, but truly magical. I stayed and worked with Dubai Golf for 15 years, won the *Emerging Golf Destination of the World Award,* and then left the company with a great deal of achievement and a job well done.

As a token of appreciation from our Chairman at the time, HH Sheikh Ahmed bin Saeed Al Maktoum (also Chairman of Emirates Airlines), I was given an honorary life membership at the golf courses—I could play golf free of charge on some of the most prestigious golf courses on the European Tour for the rest of my life! I felt appreciated, rewarded, and complete.

Life is full of surprises

I had what I thought was a wonderful marriage, two amazing children, and had worked my way up through hardship, using fierce courage, perseverance and faith. I felt that I could now spend my time on what I loved the most: Energy Work. I was helping as many people as I could; using my time building a new and different business, and getting ready to become a professional kinesiologist.

Life, however, decided that I had still some growing to do in terms of developing my spiritual muscles.

Standing Up with Courage and Faith

I was in Lebanon on a short trip when I received the phone call that changed my life: my husband was having an affair with someone I knew. Talk about being "bombed in Lebanon!" Not only had he decided to leave us without any warning, but he also chose not to talk about it. He abandoned the family business, which I found in bad shape, and told his 16-year-old son that he was now in charge of his mother and his sister. I looked for anger in me for weeks, but did not find it. What I found was deep, deep sadness.

Call it bad karma, a nightmare, accelerating growth or "show now what you are made of"—all were probably true. I knew I could not look for anything outside my world, and that I needed to rebuild from there. For the sake of my children and my sanity, I took over the family business. I put on the boots, the hardhat, and the coveralls, and I went onto oil rigs to learn what the air-conditioning business in the Oil & Gas and Marine industries was all about.

It was difficult to win the respect of our 60 engineers and workers. Imagine: six nationalities, two warehouses, no communication between them, no vision, no mission statement nor values, no processes or management systems in place, and alarming results. I rolled up my sleeves and put the business immediately on track towards ISO certification to be able to bid for bigger projects. I reinstalled my husband as CEO of the company, continued the journey towards Business Excellence, and won the *Dubai Quality Award* for best-run companies after three years of change management. I put my husband on stage to receive the award in front of 1,500 people.

I came to realize that he was tired, had enough of responsibilities, and could not talk about it. He found what he needed outside the marriage, as he could not communicate his needs and what he was longing for. He did not know that he was our rock, that we loved him beyond measure, and that we would be there for him, in sickness and in health, if only he had been courageous enough to ask for what he needed. I made a conscious choice then to love him wherever he was, to be there for better and for worse, and honor my wedding vows.

I turned the company around, found a buyer, and sold it for several million dollars three years ago. I am grateful he can think about retirement without a worry for money. I wish him well with his new choices. I am happy with my soul for showing love and kindness despite the pain and the ugliness. I stood up with courage and in full faith. Cinderella's mother would have been proud!

A New Chapter

Spring always returns, bringing its hope. Over the years, I learned the art of sales, marketing, business, and leadership. From my unique life's path, today I am a business owner, investor, and good human being. What I have learned throughout my seasons has led me to the synergy of my life today. I feel so blessed to have been of service and to have transformed many lives by what I do today.

I sometimes wonder what my life would have been if I had not sold my saxophone, taken that plane, and learned the business language of this world? The world truly changes when we change. The world shows us heart when we stay in our own heart and I have learned that the real language of it all is truly, love. "It is the Heart that heals; it is love that heals," a Great Teacher once told me.

We need never be tempted to feel that we are unfortunate, unhappy victims of the tyranny of sadness. I believe it is not what you do; it is who you are when you are doing it that changes it all. So, my question to you is:

Will you have the courage to live a magical life in tune with the natural pulse of your seasons and live happily ever after?

Success Strategies

1 I believe the reason you have a childhood is to have something to work on when you grow up! *Welcome all experiences.* Forgive and Forget! It is not about who is right or who is wrong; it is about doing the right thing.

2 Work on *your relationship;* don't look elsewhere.

3 A great relationship is not where you go and get something, it is where you *give something.*

4 Success is not to be superior to others; success is to be superior to your *former self.* Expectations make us unhappy. Trade your expectations for *appreciation* and your life will truly change.

5 Work to *express,* not to impress. Strive for improvement instead of perfection. It is never what you do, but rather who you are when you are doing it.

6 Wear the shoes! Decide to create *spectacular* every day. When you look around, life is pretty amazing!

7 Everything will be okay at the end, and if it is not okay, then it is not 'THE END!'

Beth Gardner

Beth graduated from the French Culinary Institute in 1999 with a *Grande Diplôme* in Classic Culinary Arts and has plied her trade as *Chef de Cuisine* in critically acclaimed restaurants around the world—most notably in France and Israel.

Before her most recent position of 10+ years as a Test Kitchen Director, Beth established a highly successful business as a private chef and caterer, with clients in New York City, Martha's Vineyard, and Connecticut.

Most recently she received her Masters of Science in Human Nutrition, *summa cum laude,* from the University of Bridgeport. Beth also conducts cooking classes and demonstrations nationwide and is an active member of several culinary associations.

SECTION 2: CHAPTER 3

Open

by Beth Gardner

"A mind is like a parachute. It doesn't work if it is not open." Frank Zappa

As the wheels of the plane touched down at JFK, I felt a slight wave of anxiety come over me. The whirlwind work tour started in Jamaica and ended six days later in Trinidad. Every moment of my trip, when I was not working, was spent with my class notes in hand, studying like my life depended on it. Now, I was headed home and knew the craziness would continue. It was already 11:00 p.m. and reality was setting in. I still needed to collect my bag and get through Customs before I could even think of the hour-plus drive home. Was I really going to make it through the weekend? First thing the following morning, I had an exam in Anatomy and Physiology.

The next day, I not only had an exam in Biochemistry, but also a ten-page term paper due that I had not exactly finished. To top it all, I had an 18-month-old baby at home with a host of allergies, and a failing marriage. Sounds like fun, doesn't it?

This snapshot sums up a two-year chapter in my life when chaos ruled. But this story, as you will see, is not about the fact that my life was in a state of chaos (I will reserve that for a different book). Instead, this story is about what I learned through different life experiences. They helped to unlock my inherent open nature and allowed me to develop in a variety of ways. Ultimately, those encounters and my new-found openness gave me the tools to take on any of life's challenges thoughtfully and with confidence.

Even with the constant juggling during that two-year period—the late nights, the studying in the car trying my best to comprehend biochemistry while not crashing into the car in front of me—I did it. I found the strength to raise a child on my own, excel at my job, and still graduate *summa cum laude* with my Masters of Science in Human Nutrition.

I could list a number of attributes that define me and which could easily explain the secret to my success, but the one I keep coming back to is 'open.' And, when I say *open,* I really mean it in every sense of the word: overall living with an open mind and an open heart; open for adventure and all that comes with it, like new experiences, opportunities, and risks; keeping one's options open; open to suggestions; and, finally, open with relationships, both professional and personal.

Many of life's twists and turns helped to cultivate my ability to be open and to take on any situation headfirst. I was very fortunate to have had the opportunity to do some extensive traveling earlier in my life. Three adventures in particular helped me to develop personally, spiritually, and professionally. Each one was a time where I pushed the envelope and went far outside my comfort zone. Because of what these experiences taught me, I have been able to face any event with poise—turning my most chaotic moments into success.

Australia

My first traveling adventure was a semester abroad in Australia during my junior year in college. It started on the drive to LAX as panic was bubbling beneath the surface. The idea of traveling across the world to Cairns, Australia, and meeting 19 strangers with whom I was to spend the next four months was slightly overwhelming—especially to a girl who would be considered rather introverted. However, as it turned out, the panic that was slowly building on the three-hour drive from Santa Barbara almost immediately disappeared once I met some of the kids in my group at the airport. The 18-hour plane ride actually helped, as it became a group bonding fest that immediately set me at ease.

On a park bench in Australia one memorable day, panic and anxiety hit me again. As part of our orientation, we were individually dropped off in a random town in the middle of the vast, empty Australian Outback. The purpose was to gather as much information from the locals as we could, then somehow make our way back to base and report to the group that evening. Scary was an understatement!

As we were loading into the minivan, all I could think was, *"What in the world am I doing?"* I nervously looked around at my peers and thought to myself, "Am I the only one who is absolutely terrified?" We approached the first stop and, of course, my name was called. I stepped out of the van, took a deep breath as I surveyed my surroundings, then I turned around to watch the van drive off, leaving me behind, alone. I started walking toward a park and found a bench. I spent at least 30 minutes sitting on that park bench going over in my mind the best plan of action to actually drum up the courage to speak with a complete stranger. The idea of walking up to someone and striking up a conversation was completely inconceivable to me—it was too far outside my comfort zone.

As unnatural as it felt, I decided to push myself, all the while keeping an open mind to the whole experience. I learned a powerful lesson: openness begets openness. I found that when I approached strangers in an open and friendly way, they responded in kind—they were open as well. I was not naïve enough to think that everyone would respond to me in that fashion, but, as it turned out, most of the people I met during my time in Australia were just as open as I had become. This instilled a great deal of confidence in me.

As I sat on the park bench, I could see an elementary school. I decided that would be the first stop in my exploration. The amazing thing is that as soon as I found my courage and made my way over to the school, I was welcomed instantly and put at ease by their openness. After meeting with a few classrooms, I had the chance to chat with a group of teachers over a cup of coffee. They recommended that I see an old dairy farmer who lived up the road. I loved their suggestion, thanked them for their time, and set off on the road to the farm. It was a small first step, but I could already see a change within myself.

I was beginning to see that if I remained open to people, open to ideas, and open to challenges, good things would come. The farmer's name was Tex; he had worked on the dairy farm all his life. You could see in his rugged face and in his tired body that he had lived a hard but fulfilling life. I stayed with Tex as he sorted eggs from the hundreds of hens on his farm. I felt fortunate that he allowed me into his life for a few hours. It was amazing to me that while I was on the other side of the globe, I was able to connect with people who, under ordinary circumstances, I would never have had the opportunity to meet.

When I left Tex and the farm, I started walking back down the road to the center of town. In true Australian fashion, I finished my day at the pub. I went in, struck up conversations with strangers, hung with the locals, and even found myself a ride home.

Back with my group, it was time for all of us to share our experiences of the day. I remember feeling so proud of myself and so accomplished as I got up in front of everyone to recount my remarkable day. Looking back, that day really captured my entire semester abroad. It was a turning point for me; a time when I really opened up to so many things for the first time in my life. I truly came out of my introverted shell, and that made me feel more confident in many ways.

Most importantly, that day in the Australian Outback taught me an invaluable lesson that has helped me tremendously, both personally and professionally. It taught me that when I allow myself to be open, I will be rewarded with openness from others. That was an important life lesson.

> *"To awaken quite alone in a strange town is one of the pleasantest sensations in the world."*
> Dame Freya Stark

Israel

My second traveling adventure was in Israel. At the age of 22, a medical scare left me questioning what exactly it was I wanted to do with my life in order to make it count. What better way to find out than to get out of my comfort zone once again and get on the open road to a new adventure.

I decided to go to Israel to live and work on a kibbutz (a farming settlement) to learn about my spiritual roots. Before traveling to Israel, I honestly did not feel connected spiritually in any real way. I was raised in the Jewish faith, but I never really embraced my religion nor identified myself as particularly Jewish. It took the 'Holy Land' 6,000 miles away for me to really understand the importance of knowing your origins. I can honestly say that being in Israel, a country so rich in history and religion, was the first time I experienced anything spiritual. I got a glimmer of how powerful it could be in my life.

There is something to be said for the importance of getting in touch with spirituality, regardless of your religion. When you can become spiritually grounded you are more open to success and truly grateful for opportunities that come your way. This is not always easily achieved. Even today, I strive to incorporate more spirituality in my life.

A year in Israel immersing myself in the culture and living with the people—in both a secular and religious sense—truly changed me. I was able to learn firsthand that connecting in a deeper way to my surroundings, understanding the struggles and triumphs of those who came before me, did wonders for my soul. My year in the 'mother ship' (as I affectionately call Israel) gave me a wealth of experience that taught me to be tolerant, introspective, and open to include spiritual practice in my life. It was a place where I felt at home. Although I was reluctant to leave Israel, my journey kept me open to options for my future that ultimately landed me a job offer that brought me back to the U.S. and New York City.

France

The study-abroad director position that brought me to New York City from Israel came to an end after two years. At this point, and after much thought, I decided to follow my lifelong passion in food and attend culinary school. It was an instant fit for me and for the first time in my life, I wanted to be the best at what I was doing. What better experience than to work in a kitchen in France?

The French experience was the final, defining journey for me—a six-month internship in a restaurant in the South of France which commenced immediately upon graduating culinary school. Being an American woman in a French kitchen is not for the faint of heart. Only a handful of English was spoken and we all worked like dogs—split shifts six days a week in a small, hot kitchen.

Every day, twice a day, we would walk to work up a steep half-mile incline to get to the restaurant. Young French men (supposed colleagues) would try their best to sabotage their classmates' work any chance they could get. But, I made a conscious effort to be open to the whole experience, work hard, and learn from those around me.

Respect is not given, it is earned, and I had the respect of my entire French crew. I also grew to respect myself by learning firsthand that by working really hard one can accomplish just about anything. I came back to the States with a hunger to work hard and do whatever it took to get what I wanted.

That is just what I did.

After returning to the States, I worked in restaurants for years, eventually realizing that restaurant life was not going to work for me with a family. I needed to structure my career to allow me to follow my passion for the culinary arts and also be at home with my daughter, both before and after school. I didn't want to be coming home to her at two o'clock in the morning, six days a week.

The lessons I learned from my traveling adventures about being open allowed me to seize the opportunity to mastermind a 'test' kitchen for a premier home appliance company. It gave me the confidence to pursue a career that I never knew existed. This position has turned out to be the perfect match for me and my life.

The confidence that I developed from being open during my travels has served me well in my career. It has allowed me to thrive and grow in the corporate environment.

Staying open to people, open to learning, and open to opportunities is the lesson I want to share with my daughter and with women everywhere.

"If you go out looking for friends, you're going to find they are very scarce. If you go out to be a friend, you'll find them everywhere." Zig Ziglar

Success Strategies

1. *Be open to inspiration.* Find a quiet park bench to contemplate your life and think about how being open to new people, places, or experiences could enhance your life.

2. *Be open in the moment.* Stay calm in the moment of challenge, whether in your personal or professional life.

3. *Keep an open mind.* Create a mantra that keeps you moving forward to more openness. Something as simple as, "I can do this." "I will do this." "I have done this."

4. *Be open with your heart and relationships, both professional and personal.* When you allow yourself to be open, you will be rewarded with openness from others.

5. *Be open to opportunities and adventure.* Be grateful for the experiences that result when you force yourself to move into the path of openness.

Mayra Lladó

Dr. Mayra is an architect of the smile and an architect of life. She is the author of the best-selling book, *Run Your Race: A Guide to Making Your Impossibles Possible,* as well as an International Speaker, Trainer, and Certified High-Performance Coach. Dr. Mayra is also a graduate of Jack Canfield's *Train the Trainer* program.

She is Founder & CEO of Success In Action Inc., a coaching and training company that offers High-Performance Coaching and experiential workshops for businesses and individuals. Dr. Mayra helps clients to tap into their gifts and realize their full potential, so they can change their world and the world around them.

www.mayrallado.com

SECTION 2: CHAPTER 4

Got Limits?

by Mayra Lladó

> *"Every time you state what you want or believe, you're the first to hear it. It's a message to both you and others about what you think is possible. Don't put a ceiling on yourself."* Oprah Winfrey

*H*ave you ever wanted to accomplish something that was a stretch for you and either you or somebody else decided that you couldn't do it, or have it, or be it? I remember when I was a child, my parents would put limits on me: when I could play with friends, my bedtime, what kind of foods I ate, what kind of movies I could watch, and a number of other things, mainly with my best interests in mind.

You probably remember similar constraints from your childhood. One I remember in particular was "Just because you want it, doesn't mean you can have it." That was interesting and challenging at the same time. On the one hand, my parents were very encouraging and had great faith in me. They helped me believe that I can do just about anything. They gave me many opportunities to explore different interests: playing the guitar (didn't work out); playing the violin (didn't like the teacher); playing tennis; playing on the soccer team; learning to swim in a lake (brrrr); learning to ski in snow; going on a cruise by myself with my grandmother; and so many others.

That phrase has defined how I approach many things, except that I changed it: "It is *because* I want it, that I must *find a way* to have it."

These days that applies to what I want to do, what I want to be, and what I want to have. I truly believe that anything is possible as long as you want it badly enough and are willing to take the actions necessary to get there.

Do you REALLY want it?

My mom dropped out of dental school so my dad could finish medical school and they could get married. When I was 12 years old, my mother decided she was going to go back to dental school and become a dentist as she had always wanted. I was very angry and upset with her, because this meant that we were to move from Syracuse, NY, where we had been living for most of my childhood, back to Puerto Rico.

I thought of the phrase "just because you want it, doesn't mean you can have it." My mother's story illustrates the number one element in the statement "anything is possible"—*Desire. You must want it badly enough.* Her actions demonstrated to me that she found a way to make what previously had been impossible possible—she did it because it was her burning desire.

It was because she *wanted* it, that she found a way to *make* it happen!

How do you know what you want?

You might be surprised to learn that, for many people, determining what they want is a difficult thing to decide. They have let circumstances and other people dictate what they should want, or they simply allow others to choose for them. If this sounds like you, don't despair—there are many ways for you to begin to rediscover what you desire to be, do, and have in this life. One simple exercise you can do is to answer the question, "What would you do if you had no limits?" Write down everything that comes to mind: things you would want to experience, things you would like to accomplish, things you would like to have. Remember: you have no limits of time, money, or skill.

Can you see it?

Besides knowing what you want, it is important to have clarity about the things you want to do, be, or have. Start becoming clear on what you want without putting limits on yourself. My experience has been that when I have clarity about the thing I want, I become sensitive to identifying it and see it more and more in my everyday life.

I was in the eighth grade when we moved back to Puerto Rico and my mother went back to dental school. Up to that point, I wanted to be an architect. I loved to draw pictures of houses and design their facades and other features. It was not until I witnessed my mother studying to become a dentist that I even considered dentistry as a possibility for me. My mother would wake us up every weekday to get ready for school, then would leave before anyone else because she had to be in school for her first class at 7:00 a.m. After helping us with schoolwork, dinner, and bath time, she would stay up studying many nights past 1:00 a.m. I watched her with fascination, realizing that being a dentist was like being an architect, except of the mouth, and decided that was what I wanted to do. It became so clear. That is what made it possible for me: the power of my clarity served as a roadmap. Because I loved the creativity involved in being a Prosthodontist (architect of the smile), I continued my studies to specialize in aesthetic dentistry.

How do you become clear about what you want?

Let's say you decided that you want to be financially free. That's a great goal—the challenge is that it is too broad and not specific. This makes it difficult for your mind to see it as possible because there is not a clear destination. Let's take this goal of financial freedom and clarify it by asking yourself questions to narrow it down: How will you know when you are financially 'free'? How much money are you earning? How much money do you have in savings? How much debt do you need to pay off? How often are you traveling? Where do you live?

When you know these details, then it will be clear where you want to go. Make sure you have every detail clear in your mind.

Who will you emulate?

Up until this point, my education had come from my parents and other close family members, my teachers in grade school, high school, college, dental school, my peers, and my experiences. The next logical step for me was to start my own dental practice, get married, and live happily ever after. I assure you that I did my best to do just that!

Starting my own practice meant becoming my mother's partner. Not so bad, except that I had very clear ideas on what

I wanted my dental practice to be, and my mother had already established the way she wanted her dental practice to be, and they weren't exactly the same.

Thus began my search for more. I knew that, deep down, this could not be all there is. I quickly learned that I knew very well how to treat my patients and help them feel and look better, yet I really knew nothing about running a successful business.

Entrepreneurship is a painful learning experience. I wanted to find a way to short-cut the growth of my practice so I could choose the kinds of treatments I wanted to perform, instead of feeling like I had to treat every patient who walked through the door just to pay the bills. I had ordered different programs to start other businesses that could supplement my income. A lot of them seemed promising yet complicated, plus I was also seeing patients full time. My name got on a lead list and I eventually received a letter in the mail that talked about a technology that eliminated strong odors and sanitized the environment. This piqued my interest—I thought it might help with some of the chemical odors in my dental office. This eventually led me to start a business with the network marketing company that made this product (but, remember, I knew nothing about business).

The Power of Role Models

The person who introduced me to that opportunity believed in me and showed me that many other people had succeeded in the business—and, because of that, I could succeed also, as long as I followed the system. So I did just that. And guess what? It worked! Before I knew it, I had won an all-expense paid trip to the home office for training. Here I really came to understand the power of role models and the power of belief. Without me knowing how important her role had been up to this point, my mother had already been my first role model of career success. Now I was being introduced to the most amazing and limitless world I could have ever imagined. I had the power in my mind to decide what was possible and what was not—it was all up to me!

This was my first exposure to personal development. The first book I read was by John C. Maxwell, then others by Dale Carnegie and Napoleon Hill. I was hooked! This business had introduced me to something I never new existed: the human potential movement. I learned and understood that I could be, do, and have anything I set my mind to. I learned that our thoughts are powerful and that everything that exists began as just a thought.

Role models can help you with your faith and belief in yourself. I looked to the people who were already successful in the business to teach me and share with me how they had done it. As Tony Robbins says, "Success leaves clues." This built my confidence and faith that I could also be successful in business—and in a totally new and different one at that!

Finding role models can be fun! You can find them in books, in your community, in your social network, in your family, among your peers, or online. It all depends on what you want to do. Find someone who is already where you want to be. This way you can start thinking like them, acting like them, and finally becoming the best version of you in the process of getting to your destination.

Struggle is Part of Success

I was able to build an incredibly successful business and be in the top 10 of my company several years in a row, made it to the Millionaire Circle, and had the opportunity to coach and train thousands of individuals on how to become successful in our business. You might be thinking, "Oh, that was her and everything seems to come easy for her" or "my situation is different."

The truth is, it was not easy, and many times the thought crossed my mind that maybe it was not going to work for me—that I was wasting my time. I remember during one of those moments when I was ready to quit, I heard one of my mentors talk about how achieving success is like the transformation that occurs to a caterpillar in order for it to become a butterfly. He mentioned that the caterpillar has to break out of the cocoon by himself in order to become the amazing butterfly it is meant to become. Each one has their own struggle to go through in order to fulfill their destiny of becoming a butterfly.

That is when I knew that struggle was an important ingredient to my success. It was because I wanted to have more freedom in my dental practice that I found a way to make it happen. I had the desire, I had the role models, I had the belief in myself...and the last thing I had was the element of possibility: I was open to better outcomes.

Be Open to Better Outcomes

It is important to have a clear and specific intention, as I have mentioned already, yet not be attached to the result. Rather, be open to the possibility of an even better outcome than you could have imagined. This does not mean giving up on your goal—it means just the opposite. It is being committed to it, taking the necessary actions towards it, and being open to achieve and experience something even better.

This has happened to me in many instances. When I was writing my first book, I had the goal and intention to finish the first draft by the end of 2012. I had high intentions with regards to finishing by that date, yet I had decided to not be attached to the date. In other words, I would do everything possible to get it done by then, but would have faith that if it didn't happen, that it was an opportunity for more.

I ended up finishing my manuscript towards the end of April and because of that was able to include two very inspirational and important stories that strengthened the message I wanted to communicate.

By not forcing the issue and being open to better outcomes, my book was much more impactful.

My husband, Antonio, and I had the goal and desire to take a Mediterranean cruise even before we got married. I had a picture of one on my vision board for several years. Last year the opportunity presented itself. Our very good friends were having a destination wedding on the Island of Santorini, Greece. The wedding was to take place on June 16th, 2014. We decided we could plan to go on a Mediterranean cruise after the wedding. I contacted a good friend who lives in Greece to see if we could visit while we were there. She immediately asked if we could come sooner than we planned since she had a special event scheduled on May 30th that she would love for us to attend.

By changing our travel dates to two weeks earlier, we saved over $2,000 in travel expenses. The best part was that because of the change we were also able to visit Venice. The outcome could not have been better! We had an incredible time in Athens at *The Better Life Day,* we met our friend's husband, Nicholas, and we spent time with other friends who were participating at the event. We then flew to Rome to explore and then board our cruise. After the cruise, we took a train to Venice to see the uniqueness of transportation via waterways and finished our journey the best way possible: sharing in our friends' special wedding on the magical Island of Santorini.

If you haven't had an experience like the ones I mentioned before, I want to challenge you to have high intention and low attachment to the deadline or end result next time you are working on accomplishing a goal. Notice how you feel and remember to be open to better outcomes, even if it takes a little longer.

It is my mission to share the possibilities we all have within ourselves to be, do, and have that which we most desire. Now go out and make the impossible possible! "It is because you *want it,* that you must find a way to *have it.*" I believe in you and can't wait to hear your story of possibility!

"Don't limit yourself. Many people limit themselves to what they think they can do. You can go as far as your mind lets you. What you believe, remember, you can achieve." Mary Kay Ash

Success Strategies

1. Be clear on what it is you want and that it is *your desire,* not somebody else's.

2. Find *Role Models*—people who have gone before you and paved the way.

3. Have *faith* that it is possible for you. Remember your thoughts are powerful.

4. *Struggle* is part of success.

5. Be open to *better outcomes.* This is the ultimate non-limiting approach.

Amanda Brown

Amanda has been training in and researching human potential techniques for over a decade. Now, as a transformational trainer and international speaker, she has founded The Leading Ladies Company. Her work has led many people to step outside their day-to-day routines to create phenomenal lives for themselves and their families.

A comment from a friend a few years ago—"There must be more to life than this"—was a catalyst for Amanda to create '*The LIPSTICK Principles*™' success strategies for women. Amanda has also founded the inspiring Leading Ladies TV channel where women share their stories of life to inspire other women around the globe.

www.theleadingladiescompany.com

SECTION 2: CHAPTER 5

Feedback - How to Receive a Standing Ovation

by Amanda Brown

> *"Feedback is the breakfast of champions."*
> *Ken Blanchard*

*A*s I ran from the room my bottom lip was quivering and I was in tears. It was an Oscar-winning performance in my show, and I played the scene beautifully. I was not on stage, I was not taking directions from anyone. I was simply having a personal reaction to some feedback that I had received.

Why is some feedback so hard to hear?

The leading ladies of stage and screen continually receive feedback. That is exactly how they perfect their scenes, and master their craft. The successful ones have learned how to take the feedback and use it to improve their performance.

We may not be theatrical performers, but we are all leading ladies in our own show of life. We have no understudies, and sadly we have no rehearsal time. Whatever comes our way, we know that the show must always go on.

Our performance in our show starts from the moment we are born, through to the final curtain. Each day we can choose whether to make it a memorable, awe-inspiring performance or an average one.

Recently I went to watch a fabulous stage production of The Lion King®. The energy and enthusiasm of the cast was amazing. They were performing twice a day to a packed theatre, yet were able to give the same energy to each show as though it were the first. At the end of the show, the audience rose to their feet to give the cast the feedback they deserved: a standing ovation. Imagine if the feedback on our performance each day was a standing ovation!

While on my journey towards making a success of my show, I have developed some strategies that have helped me to quickly and effectively improve my performance.

Catch the Compliment

Do you feel uncomfortable when you are paid a compliment?

I can remember years back when I was in my teens, my mum had a lovely friend named Gillian who was very attractive. She was always beautifully made-up, well-dressed, and wore quirky and interesting jewelry. She was one of the nicest people you could hope to meet, and was always the first to compliment anyone.

I asked mum one day how Gillian was, and was really surprised when mum told me that she thought Gillian had very low self-esteem. Mum went on to explain that whenever she tried to pay Gillian a compliment, whether it be about her hair, an outfit she was wearing, or just how good she was looking, Gillian would always bat it away with comments such as, "This old thing? It was really cheap," or "My hairstyle is so old fashioned" or "I look really ugly compared to you." She would always downgrade the compliment. Any praise made her feel uncomfortable, and sadly, she unconsciously made Mum feel uncomfortable, too.

After a while, Mum stopped trying to pay her any compliments. Why should a compliment make someone feel uncomfortable? After years of research, development, and training, I now recognize deflecting compliments is one of the ways that low self-esteem shows itself.

When I was in my late twenties I went through an intense period of self-doubt, not feeling good enough, and believing that everyone else was better than me. I had a best friend who would always pay me compliments. One day as she complimented me on a coat I was wearing, I began to tell her some story about the coat being on sale. My friend threw her hands in the air and said, "Stop, Amanda. Don't do it!" She went on to tell me that she didn't want to hear anything about the coat being old, half-price, or anything else. "Please just take the compliment. I love your coat."

I was shocked, and then the penny dropped. I realized that due to my own low self-esteem, I had gotten into the habit of deflecting compliments, as my Mum's friend had done years before. By doing so, I was also upsetting my friend.

When I am working with clients who are striving towards making a success of their performance in life, I usually ask the question, "How well do you receive compliments?" Most will not have a problem with it, but there are many who admit they feel very uncomfortable with accepting compliments. It is almost as though when given a compliment the leading lady leaves the stage and is replaced with a baseball player who is up to bat, pulling back the bat as the compliment comes close, ready to whack it away.

Success Strategy 1

Catch the compliments with both hands, hold them to your heart and feel them.

The strategy I developed for catching the compliment is to picture being a baseball player, not up to bat, but out in the field. I would be prepared to catch any compliment that came my way. I would imagine holding my arms out to catch it, and when I had it in my hands I would pull it right down and hold it tight, just by my heart. As I held it there, I heard it, I felt it, and I said, "Thank you." It was a challenge at first not to say anything more than thank you, not to add my own twist. It took quite a bit of practice, as does everything that we want to perfect about our performance. "Thank you" is all you need to say when you receive the gift of a compliment.

I received a note from a wonderful lady with whom I had shared this strategy. It read, "Dear Amanda, I have turned into a baseball player. I am catching compliments and holding them dear. With the first few that I imagined grabbing, nothing happened. Then I caught one and held it close, I felt it in my heart, and I actually had tears in my eyes. The compliment came from my husband, and as I looked at him and thanked him, I realized that I had been batting away his compliments for a long time. We had a hug, the first one in months, and it felt fantastic."

> *"Feedback is a gift, accept it in the present, and as a present."* Amanda Brown

Notice the people around you on a daily basis, and observe the essence of people who catch and accept their compliments.

Once I had mastered catching the compliments, my self esteem began to rise. However, I still doubted myself. Even though I could now accept compliments from others, I would secretly be putting myself down. I was still giving myself a constant stream of negative feedback on my performance. I wonder now, looking back, how I ever achieved anything while I was in this mind set. This was the next thing that I needed to change. How could I ever hope to achieve anything, when all the time I was telling myself that I never would? I developed another strategy that really helped me along the road to success.

Success Strategy 2

Become your number one fan and the director of your own successful performance.

This I call my 'WINning Strategy.' I had to find a way to appreciate myself and all that I was achieving as well as acknowledge and learn from what I was not doing so well. Each night I began implementing this strategy. My WINning Strategy looks like this:

W *ell Done!*   What has gone well for me today?

I *ndifferent*   What has not gone so well?

N *ext time*   What would I do differently?

Each night I would review my day and see what had been a success. I would then pay attention, for a moment, to what had not gone well, then quickly move on to what I would do differently next time. Within days of implementing this strategy, my thought patterns changed. My whole being changed. Suddenly, I realized that I was a winner and not a loser at all. I felt that I had control of my life, my outcomes, my results, and most importantly my thoughts. I still use this strategy every day; it works so well for me. An example of my WINning ritual would look like this:

*W*ell Done! *What has gone well for me today?*

My coaching call this morning was great, I had a lovely lunch with my friend, I finished the chapter for the book, I did my one-hour work out, and I even managed to read a few chapters—Well Done, proud of you today, Amanda!

*I*ndifferent *What has not gone so well?*

I didn't make the call to the bank. I didn't get to spend much time with my partner. I was frustrated about how long the chapter took to write, and got upset with myself about it.

*N*ext time *What would I do differently?*

I will make the call to the bank my first job of the day. I will turn everything off when my partner comes in, and discuss his day. I will appreciate myself for all that I achieved and not beat myself up about what I didn't.

Giving myself feedback each day helps me to improve my performance, and takes the emotion away from what I didn't get right.

I recently met up with a client who I taught this strategy to five years ago. She has grown her business 55 percent over the last five years, and she told me that she still uses my WINning Strategy. She has adopted the strategy to use with her team at work as a way of reviewing progress. Her team loves it, and she said that it has helped them and the business enormously.

The next step towards becoming the shining star of our show is being prepared to face our critics. This is the step that had me running from the room with my lip quivering and tears rolling down my face.

> *"Critics are our friends, they show us our faults."*
> *Benjamin Franklin*

We need to know our blind spots and be able to appreciate what other people see. Family and friends do not always make the best critics as they are often reluctant to share feedback with us, for fear of hurting us. But if they can see ways in which we could improve our performance, or notice behaviours or repeating patterns which could be limiting us, then they hold valuable information.

For the brave and the bold, and those who are truly dedicated to success, I will share my next success strategy.

Success Strategy 3

Invite those that know us well to give us feedback on our performance.

Ask these questions: "Where do you think I could improve? What, specifically, do you think I could do better? Do you see me limiting myself at all? What do you see me doing when I am performing at my best? What do you think I do well?"

It was when I asked a group of friends the third question that my Oscar-winning performance happened. I ran from the room, my bottom lip quivering and tears pricking my eyes.

These friends knew me so well and loved me enough to actually tell me the truth. Yet it was so hard to hear. Four people told me the same thing, and pointed out something in me that they saw as limiting behaviour. The fact is that once it had been pointed out to me, and I had taken the time to think about it, I recognized that they were right.

The feedback that they generously gave me that day made me aware of something that had been holding me back, and as it was something I could change, it actually transformed me. We all know that truth can often hurt. However, wouldn't you rather know? The feedback I received that day took a blind spot away and helped me grow at a rapid speed which wouldn't have been possible without accepting that feedback. If we are the only ones blissfully unaware of our limitations, then we will remain limited.

In order to grow faster, we have to get more feedback, get it often, learn from it, and, of course, welcome it as the gift that it is.

I have perfected receiving feedback now with practice. I thank the gift provider and receive it in the same way as a compliment—catch it, pull it into our heart, and grow from it. Everything becomes easier with practice.

> *"Feedback is a gift. It is your choice whether you accept it and unwrap it."* Amanda Brown

Feedback is only the opinion of one person over another. If only one person had shared the limitation they saw in me that day, I could potentially have dismissed it.

But when four people said the same thing, it was time for me to hear it.

After a talk I delivered recently, a lady told me that she had not liked one particular analogy I had used. I thanked her for her feedback. That evening I received many compliments and comments on the talk from other members of the audience, all whom had particularly loved the analogy I had used, and said that they had found it really motivating. I decide to let the first comment go, as it did not match the rest of the feedback.

Just because a gift is given, it does not mean that we have to use it. I have also mastered asking for feedback at a time when I am willing and receptive to receive it.

Last year I was launching a new business. I had many sleepless nights and was feeling the stress on launch day, as things did not go according to plan. A friend called and asked if I would like him to give me some feedback on the new website. I thanked him and said that I would really welcome it, but could we schedule a time for the following week. I knew that on that particular day, the last thing I needed was even well-intentioned, constructive feedback.

"I needed the love and not the lesson on that day."
Amanda Brown

The Standing Ovation

Last week, I ran a training event and asked the question, "Who has never received a standing ovation?" Around 20 hands went up. My next question was, "Who would like to receive a standing ovation?" Half the hands went up. Not everyone wanted one or felt like receiving one. The whole group then gave those that wanted it a standing ovation, and they loved it. A standing ovation does feel amazing, and we all deserve a standing ovation for our performance every day.

The next time you are among friends, I invite you to share with them the analogy in this chapter. Share with them that you are all leading ladies in this show we call life. Then, one-by-one, invite each of them to take their place in front of everyone and receive a standing ovation for their life performance. When you are ready and you want your own standing ovation for all the hard work you do everyday, how far you have come, what you have learned, and for being the leading lady in your show, simply turn to your friends and ask.

Success Strategies

① *Catch the compliment.* Don't bat it away, but rather catch it, hold it to your heart, and feel it deeply.

② *Use the WINning Strategy* to become your number one fan. Each night, review your performance and ask:

Well Done! What went well for me today?

Indifferent What could have gone better?

Next Time What would I do differently?

③ *Ask for feedback.* Don't take it personally. Accept it as you would a compliment and use it to improve your performance.

④ *Accept feedback only when you are ready.* Just because someone offers you a gift, doesn't mean it's the right time to open it.

⑤ *Receive and give standing ovations!* Celebrate successes in life!

Jean Ann Reuter

Jean is CEO & Founder of TrainPeople.com, Inc., a training and consulting firm specializing in developing online learning programs focused on change management, process improvement, and systems implementation.

In addition, she teaches corporations how to bring joy, passion, and productivity back into the workplace through her Heart Center Workplace skill workshops.

Jean is a best-selling author and winner of the *Mom's Choice Award* for her children's book, *Oodles of Love—The Power of Pawsitive Thinking.*

Jean brings her message of positive thinking to schools through her DARE to be Positive Program.

www.trainpeople.com

SECTION 2: CHAPTER 6

Determination + Persistence = SUCCESS

by Jean Ann Reuter

> *"Patience, Persistence and Perspiration make an unbeatable combination for success."* Napoleon Hill

Take a leap of faith

As a young girl, I was shaken to my core—questioning who I was and questioning my own abilities. I was told "you are not smart enough," "you are not good enough," "you are too shy," "you are too short," and "you are too weak." The lists of *'too this'* or *'too that'* seemed to go on forever.

As children, many of us begin to believe what we are told. However, as shaken as I was, I came out of this totally unshaken, full of faith, and with the belief that I *am* smart enough, I *am* good enough, I *am* strong, I *am* just right the way I am.

As a child, and even later in life, all odds seemed to be against me. So how did I become an independent thinker, a successful business woman, and a best-selling author? It was one memorable event in my early childhood which drove me to realize the qualities that were held inside my soul: it took place one day at my local swimming pool when I was about eight years old. Up until that time, I believed everything everyone told me. However, the adventures of that day gave me unshakeable faith in myself.

My father, more of a Marine Drill Sergeant than a father at times, had a goal that all of his children would learn how to swim, come hell or high water. Don't get me wrong; I loved my dad. My sister, brother, and I were in Dad's swimming classes as early as I can remember and I had learned how to swim and dive off the short board very well. But, on this particular day, my whole family and I headed to the high dive. Even though my dad had been prepping us for weeks, the high dive seemed untouchable. With all I had been told by my parents, teachers, and friends, I kept thinking, "I *am* too weak, too short, too little, too scared to do this." Still, my father demanded I go to the high dive and jump.

Trembling and fearful, I went to the bottom of the high dive stairs. I stood at the bottom and looked up, feeling nothing but fear running through my entire body. I felt frozen—all of the other kids were yelling at me, "Move it, Shorty." I stood there looking up in fear…and, while clutching the rails, began to think, "you are doing this," "you can do this," "you are strong," and *"you can absolutely do this!"*

Slowly and gingerly I climbed the stairs step by step. I made it to the top and continued to coach myself: "You can do this." At the top, I stood holding the railings as tightly as I could, shaking. Kids were still heckling, dad was screaming, "Let's go! *Jump!*" At this point, I took a deep breath then started to walk slowly, letting go of the handles. The board moved up and down as I walked my tiny body to the edge. I was shaking with fear. Again I said to myself, "I *can* do this; I *will* do this…I *am doing this,*" as I quickly held my nose and jumped.

I could not believe I actually jumped. I came to the surface with a huge smile on my face, giggling all the way. I had convinced myself I could do something. *This was the day I realized I could do anything as long as I had faith in myself.* This was when my journey of unshakeable faith, perseverance, and belief in myself began.

Challenges Strengthen Your Successes

As I went through life, I faced fears, roadblocks, and impossible feats. At times, all I wanted to do was quit. Still, there has always been something inside of me that kept saying, "Keep going. You can do this. Good things are coming to you."

From an early age I always had a desire to succeed: I wanted to go to college, be a teacher, succeed in the business world, own my own business, and be a best-selling author. I believe that when the odds were against me, those were the times I excelled the most. What was it that kept me going? *Persistence* was key. I never gave up on my dreams, goals, and desires. I always had a desire to make available for myself the best life possible. Throughout my experiences, I've had a great many people who said 'no' to me. They would tell me, "You can't go to college," "It is too risky to own your own business," and "What makes you think you can write?"

You need to think for yourself, do your research, and find any way possible to make your dreams a reality.

This was not always easy for me. On my quest to go to college, my parents kept telling me I did not have enough money or all the courses needed. Yes, this was true, but my desire far outweighed what they were telling me.

I signed up at a community college and took the courses I needed, lived at home for the first two years, and worked two jobs to earn the money I needed. The odds were against me, but a strong desire and *persistence* led me to my dream university and my Bachelor of Science degree in Education.

The word 'persistent' comes from the Latin verb *persistere* which means, 'to continue with strength.' Persistence means to never give up. The longer you hang in there, the greater your chances something will happen. No matter how hard your challenges seem, the longer you persist, the more likely you are going to succeed.

Persisting Through Life's Transitions

Transitions in life can be difficult, but there is always something on the other side waiting to help you flourish. There have been many transitions throughout my career, but the biggest was transitioning from being a school teacher to working in the business world.

I loved being a school teacher, but there was a little voice inside me saying, "Branch out; there is another chapter waiting for you." I wanted to see the world, expand my reach, and have financial independence.

Reading *The Wall Street Journal*® and *Money*® magazine became a daily routine to search for the answer to my big question: "What could I do in the business world?" In 1984, there it was right on the front cover of *Money*® as if it were a message just for me: *Teachers Needed for the Personal Computer Boom!* Well, that struck excitement within me.

Now came the biggest search of my career: a company to hire me as their trainer to teach computers. Did I have experience with computers? No, not one little bit of computer knowledge. So it quickly became my job to learn everything I could and then convince the business world that I would be the best trainer to help them teach computers to their employees.

Knocking on many doors and living through the experience of many job interviews, I heard the same message over and over, "we are looking for someone with business experience" or "we need someone with a business degree" or "we are looking for someone with a computer science background."

During this time there were quite a few jobs for trainers available. Every interview was a 'no', yet I would not take 'no' for an answer. In the depths of my heart, and deep down in my soul, I knew that this was the right move for me. Learning more about computers became a passion.

As I continued to interview, it became easier for me to talk about my inexperience because I was now able to use computer lingo, a language that was solely self-taught. Highlighting this ability to master a field completely on my own actually helped me to secure several interviews.

My 'yes' finally did come after a series of phone calls, interviews, and disappointments. Eventually I was hired by a computer retailer and became their corporate trainer, teaching their clients on personal computer software packages. This was a true life-changing position, for it tripled my salary in one year. Sales also became a new skill of mine that tripled my salary once more.

The work I put into this transition was not easy, but I was never going to give up my quest.

My unshakeable faith, persistence, and belief that I could succeed brought me to where I am today as CEO and Founder of my own training consulting firm where we have been teaching computer software applications to corporations for over 30 years.

Never Give Up

As an individual who has mastered persistence, I am able to work through challenges, deal constructively with failures and adversity, and achieve the goals I have set for myself. It's a lot like participating in a triathlon: the triathletes who make it to the finish line are the ones who persist in practicing, learn to anticipate slumps and pace themselves, engage in positive self-talk during tough times, take steps to effectively prevent and treat injuries, and adjust expectations to fit reality—even if finishing means having to walk the last mile.

Throughout history there have been many individuals who never gave up on their dreams. One distinguishing trait these people had in common is that they all had amazing perseverance and persistence. Most of them failed repeatedly before they experienced success. However, persistence—*an internal drive for success* and a 'never give up' attitude—defined their life and their work. Here are some examples:

· Oprah Winfrey was fired from her first television job because she was 'unfit for TV.'

· The University of Southern California School of Theater, Film and Television rejected Steven Spielberg three times.

· Jerry Seinfeld was booed off stage during his first stand-up comedy routine.

· J.K. Rowling was a divorced, single mother on welfare when she wrote the Harry Potter book series.

As I started my own business, many roadblocks, obstacles, and complications came my way. Multiple times I fought through despair. I was divorced just months before I started my business. Everything I had been taught told me that I needed to play it safe because I had just bought a house and a new car.

My drive to exceed my own expectations was the force behind me. Again, a voice inside kept saying, "Branch out; there is another chapter waiting for you." Once more, when I told others of my plans to start my own business, many said things such as, "You need the security of a job" or "You know nothing about starting your own business" or "It will be a risky endeavor."

Jumping off the high dive as well as throughout my career, *taking risks and believing in myself has always gotten me where I needed to go*—what would make this next challenging journey any different?

One day, a computer programmer friend asked me if I wanted to help with a systems implementation. As we talked, this person convinced me to break out on my own. The universe works in mysterious ways—I had been looking for something, had a desire, and BAM—there it was. This was a fabulous and challenging project that brought me great insight and provided the experience I would soon need in order to gain new clients.

As with any consulting project, it came to an end and I was faced with finding my next project. However, I did not realize how difficult it would be to find clients who needed my services. As I faced my fear, I began to telemarket to potential new clients—every day for three months, I called at least 50 potential new clients and followed up with just as many. Just like in the past, I knew that even though I received many 'no' responses, I knew a 'yes' eventually would come my way.

During this trying time there were many moments when I thought of applying for a job instead of searching for new clients. Yes, it would have been easier, but I have never been a person who looked for the easy way out. I truly believe there are greater rewards when we go after something that takes a bit of work.

At this time, there was no Internet nor social media; even email was limited. I continued day after day, calling, sending letters, sending marketing materials, and doing promotions. One of the promotions was to send 'Forget Me Not' seeds to everyone who showed an interest in my services. These seed packets were sent in the spring with my business card attached, along with a letter to remind my potential clients that I was here to help them with their next project.

I kept calling, kept following up, and kept believing. Then one day, about a month after my 'Forget Me Not' promotion, I received a call from a very large corporation. They mentioned my tenacity of continued follow up and my seeds. I signed a contract with them three weeks later and they remained my client for over 15 years. Once again, a 'yes' did appear and brought more business than I could have ever imagined. This one account gave me the ability to hire over 10 employees to help with the project.

Sometimes 'yes' takes a long time to show up; it does not happen overnight. *If you act on your goals, keep going with tenacity, and never ever give up, many gifts of success will come to you.*

Success takes Patience

Many successes in my life have been accomplished by being persistent and staying the course. *Being patient and knowing what you desire is half the battle.*

It took me over 30 years to write my first children's book; it stayed in the back of my mind for that many years. I have to admit that there were many times when I was ready to give up and think I would never write it.

Whenever I am ready to give up, I think about the Giant Bamboo tree: do you know how long it takes for the Giant Bamboo to grow as tall as a building? During the first four years, the tiny plant is watered and fertilized, but nothing happens. Then, in the fifth year, it shoots up to the sky, and in six weeks the bamboo grows to 90 feet tall. If the Bamboo was not watered for any of those five years it would have died. So what was happening through those long five years: an enormous network of roots was developing to support the Bamboo's future growth.

Growth takes patience and persistence. Every drop of water makes a difference; every step you take makes an impact. You may not see the change right away, but growth is happening. William Ernest Henley penned the following (and it resonates with me every day): "I am the master of my fate and the captain of my soul." It is up to you to act on your desires, strip away your fears, stay steady, believe you can, and listen to your heart and soul.

I now realize as I stood on the high dive so many years ago, letting go of the security of the rails, inching my way slowly to the end of the board, and taking that long jump into the water, that it would be a resonating theme that continues to this day:

Let go of fear, inch your way to your dreams, and jump in with all you have!

Success Strategies

1. Listen to your heart and *believe* in yourself.

2. *Never, Never, Never* give up. A 'Yes' is always just around the corner.

3. When all odds are against you, your *desire* and *persistence* will lead you to your dreams.

4. If you act on your goals, keep going with *tenacity,* and never ever give up, many gifts of success will come to you.

5. An *internal drive for success* and a *never-give-up attitude* will define your life and your work.

6. Work through challenges, deal *constructively* with failures and adversity, and achieve your goals.

7. If you are hearing yourself say that *something needs* to *change,* change it.

8. Being *patient* and knowing what you desire is half the battle.

Success Strategies

9. *Do what you love*, do it well, and stay on track. There is always a light at the end of the tunnel.

10. *Act on your desires*, strip away your fears, stay steady, believe you can, and listen to your heart and soul.

Section 3

Smoothing Success

SECTION 3: INTRODUCTION

*O*n the road to success, life happens; the unexpected occurs and we must be prepared to handle it and keep going. Yet not everyone does—some falter or fall back; others regroup with even more tenacity and conviction and plow forward.

The authors in *Smoothing Success* are in the second category—they met life head-on and became more in the process. ***Success University for Women***™ Co-Founder *Catherine Scheers* from Canada shows us by example how to handle life's storms. Russia's *Anastasia Davidova* teaches us indomitable leadership skills.

Conversely, *Danne Reed* from the U.S. shows how strong Courageous Femininity can be. Denmark's *Lotte Vesterli* has gained much by learning to trust her Intuition, and American *Jennie Ritchie* is the embodiment of Mettle or Stick-to-it-iveness. And just to lighten things up a bit, Canadian *Carla White* shows us the value of Humour when faced with life's obstacles.

Whether you are in North America, Russia, Denmark, or anywhere in between, the principles of success still apply. These authors exemplify the principles they are sharing here with you, so that you, too, may face life's obstacles and come out swinging.

Catherine Scheers

Catherine is a professional speaker, entrepreneur, and best-selling author who maximizes employees' potential within corporations. She is Co-Founder of *Success University for Women*™ and co-author of the best-seller, *The Success Secret* (Celebrity Press, 2012). Catherine is a Jack Canfield *Success Principles*™ Trainer, Certified Professional Success Coach, and graduate of the University of Calgary.

As someone who has held several highly stressful positions, Catherine has a big heart for helping others overcome stress and reach their potential. Through her *Stress to Bliss*™ Workshops and *Blissful You*™ Spas, she helps women release their stress and re-charge their lives.

www.empoweringsuccess.ca
www.blissfulyouspa.com

SECTION 3: CHAPTER 1

Calmness in the Midst of Stress

by Catherine Scheers

> *"Life is not about waiting for the storm to pass…It's about learning to dance in the rain!"* Vivian Green

*H*ave you ever been sucker-punched in the gut by the universe? I have. It was the day after my birthday, when my husband handed me a letter that read, "Please be advised that further to our phone call yesterday, your services will no longer be required after the end of this month." Panic gripped me hard! The end of the month, and the end of my husband's contract with this oil company, was only two weeks away. We couldn't believe they would give 15 days' notice after his 15 years of service!

My emotions were roiling like a storm on the ocean—caught between terror about the future, heartbreak for my husband, helplessness at the economy and the oil crash, self-blame that I hadn't anticipated this eventuality and saved accordingly, and shame that we weren't in a better position to deal with this blow. I sat stock-still, yet my emotions were buffeting me as though I was being tossed about in a boat in a storm.

I'm ashamed to tell you that when I was finally able to put words together, they weren't words of encouragement for my husband.

They were, "We're up the creek, and just lost our paddle."

Get a Grip

Sick to my stomach, my emotions were totally running the show. Then I realized that I had to STOP! Stop the emotional free-fall, stop freaking out, stop worrying about the future, and just breathe—and so I did. For the rest of that evening, my husband and I just sat, numb, commiserating, holding each other, and yes, having a bloody big glass of wine.

Ever so slowly, hope began to creep into the slew of emotions. Maybe there was a chance we could be ok? Maybe we could work this out? Then a funny thing happened: reason crept back in and a life preserver appeared.

Hold on a second—we had a contract that called for at least 30 days' notice. It wasn't much, but it was a start. It gave us one more pay period with which to get our financial affairs in order, two more weeks for Chris to find a new job, two more weeks of pay. *Getting a grip on my emotions allowed the brain to take over and begin to find logical solutions.* In contrast, letting emotions reign was totally disempowering.

Usually a practical gal, I took the next step.

Get Angry

On a scale of emotions, anger has a higher vibration than fear. After getting a grip on fear and helplessness, the next emotional wave that hit me was anger at the oil company for their callous treatment of my husband. How dare they? How could they not even tell him in person but over the phone, followed by a two-line letter of dismissal? Not a note of thanks for all his years of service. No hand-wringing over the termination. Just the facts, ma'am. He was floored, and I got mad.

Usually I pride myself on forgiving others. Yet it quickly became clear that it's easier to forgive someone who has harmed just us—it's much more difficult to forgive someone who harms the people we love. In any case, armed with anger and a head full of steam, I took charge of this new project. First things first: call the realtor; sell the house.

Don't Overreact

My logical brain, having been previously awoken, started shooting up cautionary flares. Don't overreact. Take a second; take a breath. It's easy to overreact when those emotions are rocking your world. But *this is not the best time to make major decisions*—and yet you must. How were we to navigate these rough waters ahead when my head was swimming?

Send out an S.O.S.

I immediately texted friends and family, grappling about for another life preserver. Surely they could shine a light on a solution, give us a map or coordinates to navigate the shoals ahead? Guess what? They did. Calls, emails, and texts of support started flooding in. Offers of support, job leads, even offers of money poured in. *Support is here; we are not alone in this.* Thank God.

Put on Your Life Jacket

Although I knew that the theoretical Coast Guard was coming, I was hit with another wave. Boom! Stress grabbed me by the stomach and took me down hard. I was doubled over in pain. Since my brain wouldn't shut off, I was awake half the night. I compensated the way any good sailor would: I headed straight to Starbucks for a triple skinny vanilla latte. That's three shots of espresso per drink, mixed with a ton of milk and sugar-free syrup. It's a chemical concoction that I had previously given up, but now I reached constantly for my old friend. This will get me through my day and give me clarity. If one is good, two a day is better, right? Wrong. First of all, I'm highly sensitive to both caffeine and milk. Hence the doubling over in pain. Secondly, the triple shots of caffeine sent my heart racing, exacerbating the stress with which I was dealing.

Well, if coffee wasn't helping, perhaps wine would help. So I drank a lot of it. That made my stomach way worse and didn't allow for clear thinking, either. Comfort foods—yes, that would help. I reached for chocolate like a drowning man reaching for a life preserver. That would make me feel better, right? Nope. Surely to God there were *better coping strategies,* but in the midst of my panic, I couldn't think of what they were.

By now—between the chocolate, wine, and coffee—my stomach was so swollen that I could barely get my pants on. So now, in addition to stress, I had added a wave of self-loathing. It took me a few days to realize that I was swamping my own boat, causing an internal storm when the boat was already on the verge of capsizing.

Call 911

I was drowning. What's a girl to do? Then I remembered my emergency stress kit. In most of North America, when there is an emergency, we dial 911 to get the police, fire department, and/or paramedics to come quickly. That *allows us to react quickly in times of crisis.*

No stranger to stress—we had danced many times before—I had developed a Stress 911 kit. I remembered it now and, like dialing 911, help arrived in the nick of time. There were natural stress-relieving pills that soothed my stomach; aromatherapy stress-relief essential oils; nuts and water to remind me that my brain functions best with protein and water onboard; a meditation CD to calm my mind; even a list of friends to call in case of emergency. I felt such relief! Help had arrived.

That's when it hit me: I needed a Financial 911 kit as well. What if I had a stash of cash, a file of emergency contacts and important papers, and a list of financial advisors to call when a financial crisis hit? That would have been so helpful in these early days, when we were wandering around like zombies, unable to focus or think straight.

It's easy to get down when swamped with a crisis. But now, more than ever, we needed to seek out joy. We found humour where we could, watched funny movies, told jokes, walked in nature to soothe our souls.

I've started a Joy 911 list for such times, listing 20 things that bring me joy or make me happy.

Batten Down the Hatches

Just when I thought my head was above the deep waters, I was totally swamped by yet another emotion—shame. It began almost instantly upon hearing the news, but I had managed that initial wave. Now it grabbed me and took me down hard. I was overwhelmed by support, dashed by conflicting advice, embarrassed to answer the very personal and private financial questions that well-meaning relatives were asking about our financial situation, and angry to find they had been discussing our situation amongst themselves. I was ashamed. Another wave hit! Boom! Angry again! How could they gossip about us behind our backs? I'm *never* telling them another detail.

More waves hit. This one was called isolation. Stop calling, stop asking, just let us deal with this on our own! I don't care that I sent up an S.O.S., now I want you to go away and leave us alone in our shame. I found myself snapping at those who had come to our rescue. They were confused and so was I. How could I let my emotions take over like that? My boat was listing hard to starboard.

Give up the Blame

A tidal wave hit this time—it's all my fault. It's his fault. It's their fault. God knows that someone is to blame. Who is captaining this ship, anyway?! I've heard it said that blame can be spelled B-Lame. It is disempowering, because *when you blame someone, you are giving your power to them.* You are saying that you don't have, or didn't have, a choice; you are implying that they had/have all the power over you.

I grabbed for an alternative floatation device, given to me by my mentor, Jack Canfield: E + R=O. Event plus Response equals Outcome. We can't prevent the event—in this case the termination of my husband's contract—but our response to it could definitely affect the outcome. We could either blame others, isolate ourselves and cry, or we can pull up our socks and find solutions, STAT! (Right now!)

Give up Perfectionism

Just as our storm-weary boat started to regain an even keel, a rogue wave landed squarely on our deck: perfectionism. Not only was I imperfect in my contribution to this crisis, but I wasn't handling it perfectly, either. My brain kept screaming at me, "You're a success coach, for God's sake! Can't you do better than this? You write books about stress management! How can you help others with their stress when you're freaking out? You're a big phony!"

In a recent blog by meditation guru Gabrielle Bernstein, she admitted to "losing her cool." One of her readers commented what a relief it was to hear her say that, as the reader felt like a failure for often losing her self-control. Gabby's response was that she lost her cool on a daily basis. The difference, she said, was that after spending years learning and practicing meditation, her rebound time back to "normal" was much quicker.

Aha! Another life preserver. So if a meditation teacher doesn't have to be perfect, if *success is the ability to regain your composure quickly after losing it,* then maybe it's OK not to be perfect. Beside the notion that perfect is impossible, this new definition of success helped me over that wave.

Find the Eye of the Storm

> "Just because we're in a stressful situation doesn't mean that we have to get stressed out. You may be in the storm. The key is: don't let the storm get in you."
> Joel Osteen

The eye of the hurricane is the epicentre of the hurricane. It's an oasis of calm while the storm swirls madly around it.

Meditation helps me find that center of calm. It also lowers my stress set-point—the point of inflammation or explosion. When I am meditating, I'm slower to anger, slower to snap, calmer in general, better able to think pro-actively instead of re-actively.

Grab on to Self-Compassion

Just as we discussed forgiving others, we also have to forgive ourselves for our part in the crisis. As author Jack Kornfield says, "If your compassion does not include yourself, it is incomplete."

While you need to take 100 percent responsibility for your actions, you also need to be compassionate—you did the best you could with the knowledge and skills you had at the time.

Now it's time to get new tools to deal with this crisis and prevent it from happening again.

This, Too, Shall Pass

I wish I could tell you how this story ends. I pray that, long before this book is published, I can report that my husband has secured a new, even better job. But here's what I know for sure: one way or another, we will get through this.

Storms leave as quickly as they arrive. We will emerge stronger than before—stronger as a couple because we held fast to each other, trusted each other, and rowed the boat hard when we needed to; stronger as a family because they came when we sent out the S.O.S., because we learned to trust and rely on them; and stronger financially because we got our affairs in order, made difficult decisions, took action, and emerged more financially resilient.

Develop Resilience

Just as important to me as the financial resilience is the emotional resilience. Knowing that I survived this crisis increased my self-confidence, and increased my trust that when the next storm hits (and it shall), this sailor has her sea legs!

Post-script: Hallelujah! My husband DID get another job, only two weeks later! We weathered the storm and have new tools and strategies to help us in the future.

> *"You may not control all the events that happen to you, but you can decide not to be reduced by them."*
> Maya Angelou

Success Strategies

Here are some *Words of Wisdom* that may prove useful when a *crisis* hits:

1) *Get a Grip.* Don't let emotions buffet you around.

2) *Get Angry.* It's more empowering than many of the other emotions you are feeling.

3) *Don't Overreact.* It's tempting to take any action, but use sober second thought before making major decisions.

4) *Send Out an S.O.S.* Call friends and family for help.

5) *Put on Your Life Jacket.* Stress is about to hit and hit hard. Have a variety of effective coping techniques, rather than reaching for vices.

6) *Call 911.* Have a Stress, Financial, and Joy 911 kit ready at all times. Storms happen in life; be prepared.

7) *Batten Down the Hatches.* Waves of emotion will hit you and continue to hit you long after you think they are past. Knowing that there are more waves ahead allows you to brace yourself.

Success
Strategies

(8) *Give Up the Blame.* Take responsibility for your situation, but don't blame yourself or others. Your point of power is your response to what is happening. You can control the outcome by controlling your response.

(9) *Give Up Perfectionism.* Success is the ability to regain your composure quickly after losing it.

(10) *Find the Eye of the Storm.* Practicing meditation lowers your stress set-point and helps you find the center of calm in the midst of the storm.

(11) *Grab on to Self-Compassion.* Be kind to yourself, especially when going through a crisis. "If your compassion does not include yourself, it is incomplete." (Jack Kornfield)

(12) *This, Too, Shall Pass.* You will get through this, and you will emerge stronger than before.

(13) *Develop Resilience.* This crisis will build your resilience muscle. That is the gift crisis brings.

Anastasia Davidova

Anastasia is a Couples Consultant on one of St. Petersburg's TV channels and has authored the book *Ying and Yang of Marriage,* recommended by Jack Canfield.

She began her entrepreneurial activities when she was 17 years old. By the age of 22, she had established a successful travel agency, Anastasia Travel Company. In 2013, she graduated from Jack Canfield's *Train the Trainer* course.

Anastasia has received four state commendations for the organization of government forums and conferences, and in 2014 she successfully coordinated an event for 60,000 attendees.

She has visited 25+ countries and counting, and is a happy wife and mother.

http://anastasia.travel/

SECTION 3: CHAPTER 2

Personal and Business Leadership

by Anastasia Davidova

> *"Be careful when you climb the ladder to success. You don't want to get to the top just to find it leaning against the wrong wall."* Stephen Covey

Stephen Covey describes the first part of my life in the quote above—I worked hard, got to the top at a young age, and realized that my ladder of success was leaning against the wrong wall. How did I get there?

There was a girl named Anastasia who studied well and from an early age was a leader in each game she played. To gain everything by herself, to be strong and independent, were the lessons she was always taught. She graduated from school with honors then entered university.

Her career began when she was only 17, which helped her become fully independent from her parents at an early age.

By the time she was 22, she formed her own travel company that took the dominant position in the marketplace. She got married, bought a flat, a car, and a country house.

Suddenly she paused for a moment, looked back, and realized the full horror of the situation: "At 28 years old, I'm self-sufficient, but something is very wrong." She caught herself thinking about being a robot with a program-based life—a life that had no *Life* inside. All by herself, 20 hours a day, she kept on doing *everything by herself.*

She was successful but not happy. She had a husband but no children yet—she had no time! She had absolutely nothing in common with her husband. She felt like she was running along a corridor, achieving the norms and goals, and BANG... dead end! Where to go now? She surely didn't want to live as an 'all by herself' underdog anymore, but she had no clue how to live any other way.

That is what my life looked like. I took a leave and went on a tour to the paradise of the Maldive Islands, which helped me make what was probably the first truly conscious personal decision I had ever made! *That decision changed my life.* I allowed myself to live *my* life and not pay attention to what I should do.

Two weeks of rest and thoughts in Paradise fully changed my life. However, months and even years were needed to find answers to all the questions I had and to learn how to live in a different way: to be the *leader* of my life rather than a victim of society's plans. The hardest challenge was to bring myself to change everything: to destroy all the things I had created during 28 years, start life afresh with new knowledge, and build my new life where I would be a leader.

I created an ideal picture of my life, where I was a loved and loving wife, happy mum, and successful woman, where I lived life to the fullest and travelled to the secret corners of the world. I visualized my ideal husband, heard the laughter of my children, saw myself on the beach, in the mountains, in different cities.

All the people around me were confused—where was obedient Anastasia? For the first time in my life, I was free of what was 'right' and what 'it should be like.' For the first time in my life, I made up my mind and listened to my heart and my real desires. I did things just because I (not somebody else) wanted them to come true and considered them right. The only parameter here was whether or not my actions moved me closer to my ideal picture of my ideal life.

Releasing the Old, Embracing the New

Within several days, I rented a flat for myself and moved out of my apartment, separating from my husband. I was threatened and blamed. It was difficult and very frightening sometimes, but I considered it a test of my confidence in doing what I really wanted and my readiness to start a new life.

Step-by-step, my insistence and resolution led me to the first and main prize in my life: I met the man of my dreams. Now we had our common dreams that had been real wishes of each of us separately.

The first dream that came true was our daughter. We wanted her to have blue eyes, dad's long eyelashes, olive-tinted skin, and mum's curly hair. Within a year of our relationship, our lovely daughter was born: she had blue eyes, long eyelashes, olive-tinted skin, and curly hair.

My ex-husband accomplished part of his threatening mission: I lost the business that I had built over a ten year period. People I had been working with turned against me. In no time I lost everything: client base, access to my emails, trained personnel. I suffered tremendous financial losses during the divorce. Even the number of my friends was somehow drastically reduced; not everyone was ready or was comfortable with seeing 'another' Anastasia.

I learned to live all over again: to think from a new angle, to create business, to build relationships, and to be a mother.

Learning to Delegate

"The greatest leader is not necessarily the one who does the greatest things. He is the one that gets the people to do the greatest things." Ronald Reagan

It was very hard to set up a new company—I didn't trust anyone and was sure that I could handle everything *by myself* and hire personnel only for subsidiary purposes.

Family issues turned out to be much more complicated. My new picture of life had an image of a strong man. I met him, but a new problem showed up: I realized that I had no clue how to behave with strong, purposeful men. I didn't know what to do with that strong independent style.

The blind love phase of the relationship passed and time to live a family life began. I didn't have the slightest idea how to be the manager of a company as well as a wife and mother at the same time. I spread myself thin: I fed my daughter, played with her, woke up 5-10 times at night to calm her down, and therefore didn't get enough sleep. During her nap times, I tried to work setting up a new company, but I was so tired that I was fit for nothing. By the evening I was tired to death, angry, and sad, because I had no time for anything. Another restless night was ahead, followed by the next crazy day that gave no satisfaction or happiness.

That life was much too far from my ideal picture of my life. I asked myself over and over again: why isn't it working out?

Suddenly I realized there was no need to do everything by myself—I could ask my husband and seek his advice. That was such an insight. *This was one of the wisest decisions I ever made in my life!* What is more, it made me even stronger.

"What if we hire a babysitter?" my husband Arsen asked me.

"No way!" I refused flatly. "To have a stranger at home?! How will she behave with my dear little Anastasia?"

"OK, look at it in a different light. Let's assume you hire a babysitter. What opportunities can it give you?"

"I will have time for my company, and we will have time to go out somewhere ..."

"Moreover you will have time to get enough sleep. No need to do everything by yourself. Everybody will win. You will be involved in activities you like, come back home in the evening in a good mood, and see your child. What is better for little Anastasia: to see her mum always tired and nervous or get maximum attention from a babysitter during the day, then see her mum joyful and caring?"

I thought it over and in a week found a wonderful and experienced babysitter who really cherished Anastasia. I was surprised to find that the babysitter had a good influence on Anastasia. During the day, the babysitter looked after her, played with and read to her, and took her for walks. When I came home, fulfilled from work, I had the opportunity to devote myself to my little Anastasia. She, in return, made me happy with the new skills she gained during the day.

Thanks to Arsen, I managed to sort out a mess and get one sphere of my life under control. This meant a lot to me... but it wasn't enough. It was still too far from my ideal picture of life.

For a while, work became easier. However, the amount of work and new goals increased day by day. I was buried in papers, documents, and plans. What additional development could we plan for if I could hardly cope with current tasks? I heard voices in my brain saying, "Delegate!" But how? My close assistants betrayed me in the past; delegating to them resulted in losing the business I had spent ten years building.

When I admitted that it was not *their* fault but *my responsibility,* everything clicked into place. I told myself: "There was a time when you lost everything, but it's not fatal. It's just an experience." I certainly was not ready to lose everything again, but just when I admitted that losing everything was possible and finally accepted it, it surprisingly stopped bothering me.

After that I hired personnel and went about my own planning and development duties, having delegated all the routine work to others.

Strong in Business, Soft in Love?

> *"To handle yourself, use your head; to handle others, use your heart."* Eleanor Roosevelt

One more goal was left: learning how to be a wife instead of being a *home manager.* The atmosphere at home was tense and, over time, it evolved into conflicts. I asked myself, "How can I remain a strong woman and company manager but at the same time be a loving wife and mother?" I couldn't find an answer; I didn't understand how it was possible to be strong and weak at the same time.

My thoughts ran to extremes: "What if I left my job to be just a wife and mother?" But I realized I couldn't be only a housewife—I needed social time; I needed the ability to create something meaningful and important. I tried to return home from work and play the wife role: not to be a weak woman but *pretend* to be a weak woman. That lie didn't work, either.

After discussing this with my husband, it finally became clear to me. I admitted that *I am strong,* then I relaxed and started enjoying life—giving my beloved husband an opportunity to make decisions, to protect me, and take care of me. It took time for me to become at ease. My habit of trying to control and to dictate the solutions to every problem remained. Nevertheless, I slowly learned to simply be a happy and easy-going woman beside my strong man. And, at the same time, I remained a wise leader, carefully inspiring my husband with necessary ideas.

Accelerated Success

> *"You have to be burning with an idea, or a problem, or a wrong that you want to right. If you're not passionate enough from the start, you'll never stick it out."*
> Steve Jobs

Everything fell into place piece-by-piece. The last part of my vision for my life was connected with travelling. Arsen also dreamed of hitting the road, experiencing mountains, forests, and seas abroad. So, we decided that once every four weeks we should be somewhere other than at home. The decision came, but then there was the question of how to put it into practice. We had a little daughter, jobs, and things to do at home. When our friends heard about our idea, some of them made fun of us, while others said: "It's impossible! Who ever heard of such a thing? You will lose your business!" And once we started hesitating again, we just opened our laptop and booked the flights and hotels for the next six months!

Now miracles started happening. Our work efficiency and business profit increased. In three weeks, we managed to do more than we usually did during two to three months without travelling. We had the travel deadline that helped us finish things by a certain time, as we knew that later we would get an amazing trip as a prize.

During a one-year period, we visited the Temple *Expiatori de la Sagrada Familia* in Barcelona, swam with dolphins at Curaçao Island in the Caribbean Sea, enjoyed the view of Singapore at night from the infinity pool on the 57th floor of the Marina Bay Sands Hotel, took a waterfall bath on Langkawi Island (Malaysia), travelled to Descending Dragon Bay (Ha Long Bay) in Vietnam, climbed up to the Big Buddha Statue in Hong Kong, flew over the Grand Canyon in a helicopter, had a bike tour of Central Park in New York City, surfed in California, and visited Berlin, Montenegro, and Riga.

Within two years I fully changed my world view and way of thinking. I stopped going with the flow, which was built on the dictates of society. I became a leader; *a Leader of my life.* I learned to live my own life, following my own rules and my own plans.

When you radiate confidence and inner strength, you give confidence to people surrounding you to be strong and believe in their happiness. You inspire people to dream of being happy and live to the fullest, and they follow you as a leader. *You obtain success and achievements, not just speak about them.*

Looking back, I analyze the experiences I have gained so I don't forget what life has taught me. These 'Life Lessons' are reflected in my 'Laws of Leadership' *(see my Success Strategies)* which hang on the wall in front of my bed, and which I read every night before sleeping.

Success Strategies

1) Take *responsibility* for your life.

2) Create a *clear picture* of your ideal life and fulfill it with emotions and life.

3) Believe that *everything* is possible.

4) Make decisions that are guided by your *intuition* and your *heart.*

5) Admit your *fears* – and they will leave you.

6) *Trust* people.

7) Infect people with your *dreams.*

Danne Reed

Danne inspires women to revitalize themselves and redesign their lives—to venture into courageous femininity, to celebrate who they are, and to gracefully rebel against resignation.

A successful author and entrepreneur, Danne's own journey took her from pouting over missing the party of life to dusting herself off and showing up fashionably late for it! She's passionate about showing others how to do the same in their own lives.

Her book *Fashionably Late: A Sexy Little Twist to Revitalize You and Redesign Your Life!* will be available in bookstores November 2015.

www.DanneReed.com

SECTION 3: CHAPTER 3

Courageous Femininity

by Danne Reed

> *"The most courageous act is still to think for yourself. Aloud."* Coco Chanel

"You look like trouble." My husband's quiet declaration interrupted my private musing. I glanced over to see him watching me with that knowing grin on his face, and realized that he was talking about *that* kind of trouble—the *good* kind. The kind that draws people in with the irresistible promise of something exciting to come.

As my own smile returned a silent "You know it, baby," it occurred to me that, from a man who was never stingy with his compliments, this was the nicest thing he'd ever said to me. These four little words—delivered with an undercurrent of mischief—encapsulate so perfectly the person that I want to be; the person I am when I'm truly authentic; the kind of person who draws others in with the inspiration of exciting things to come.

Maybe you're wondering what exactly I was doing that captivated him. Before your imagination kicks in, I'll just tell you. I was...*thinking*. Aww, I know, boring, right? Well, not exactly.

You see, in that moment, I was thinking about the things that I would be doing in the upcoming year that I had never done before. I would be stepping outside of my comfort zone and breaking through some of my own barriers, helping so many people to live their dreams. I was thinking about fulfilling my destiny.

In that moment, I was feeling an exhilarating mixture of vulnerability and determination, confidence and humility, fear and courage. All of that swirled together into an overall sense of *excitement.*

It was a spontaneous moment that had, ironically, been a long time in the making. A few years prior, I had reached a place in my life where I rarely felt the exhilaration that this particular blend of emotions creates. Oh, I felt the fear, humility, and self-doubt quite acutely, but the determination, confidence, and courage part of the equation had tucked tail and fled.

Somewhere along my life journey I had gotten lost. When I realized I was feeling more resentment than joy, more disillusioned than inspired, more cowardly than capable, I knew something had to change.

Being a lifelong proponent of self-education, I looked for the answers in books and classes and online programs. All of these were instrumental in helping me realize that the answers were inside of me all along. I had set out to uncover a way out of the rut I was in and discovered a path that led me straight back...to Me.

That'll Shut 'Em Up

A bit of a rebel at heart, I've always felt compelled to break through boundaries, especially into those areas where I was told "girls just don't go." In my youth, this compulsion had me climbing the tallest trees and becoming an awesome left fielder; as an adult, driving an eighteen-wheeler and becoming one hospital's first female CEO.

Many of my early accomplishments were motivated by breaking through others' perceived boundaries. *"You think I can't do that? Well, I'll prove you wrong!"*

I prided myself on having the courage to accomplish things that others thought would be difficult. After every new achievement came that moment when I knew people were thinking "Wow, she actually did it." It was intoxicating...for a short time. Then the feeling would fade and I'd be on to the next challenge!

Here's the painful admission: What I didn't realize at the time was that this mindset was ultimately 'extrinsically' focused. I may have been achieving things that were contrary to what others thought I could or couldn't do; however, I was still basing my goals on what I believed *others* were thinking rather than what I *really* wanted. In other words, motivation was coming from *outside* of myself rather than from within.

The danger of this thought virus shouldn't be underestimated, as over time it led to a state of mind where I was mostly doing things out of concern for what other people thought. Eventually, I lost sight of what I thought, what I wanted, who I truly was. The courage to overcome others' perceived challenges came easily. Finding the courage to show up as my true self—to embrace, honor, and celebrate the authentic me—was a little more difficult.

The biggest challenge we face in life is becoming truly authentic—being who we really are, not who society thinks we should be, not who our parents or friends or children or bosses think we should be. If this sounds selfish, you need to understand that denying the world of your true self is the most selfish thing you can do. Showing up as the *real* YOU is the only way to truly show courage and serve others.

If your actions aren't coming from your own heart and passions, then they're fear-based rather than courageous. As I met challenges I thought others would find impressive, the motivation was coming from a deep-rooted fear of not measuring up. When I got past trying to impress others and instead focused on impressing myself, my actions were courage-based and authentic.

> *"To stand emotionally open before the world and give of our hearts without fear of hurt or demand of reciprocity – this is the ultimate act of human courage."*
> *Brendan Burchard*

Aristotle referred to a deficiency of courage as cowardice, where an overabundance of courage is simply recklessness. There were times in my life where I had a deficiency of courage, such as the time when I chose not to stand up for a classmate who was being bullied. There were times when I had an overabundance of courage, like the time when I jumped off a bridge into a muddy-watered creek. Then there were the times when I found within me the appropriate amount of courage—like when I chose to raise my son on my own rather than stay with a violent man. The instances where I had the wrong amount of courage, whether too much or too little, usually led to a tough lesson learned. The times when I showed the appropriate amount of courage, moved thoughtfully forward even though afraid, always led to achievement and growth.

True courage requires that we first know what's important to us. What are we willing to stick our necks out for? What will we risk ridicule or financial disaster or physical danger for? When we fall down or fail, what makes us get back up and push forward? What are we willing to fight for? We rarely muster courage to take action when we don't care about the outcome.

Courage

So let's get down to it. Make a list of five times in your life when you showed true courage. It might be an incident where you stood up for yourself or someone else. It might be a time when a friend or family member needed a shoulder to lean on and you were there for them. It might be a physically dangerous situation where you risked your life to save someone else. It might be a time when you chose to quit a job that was sucking the life out of you. Write down five courageous acts.

Looking at the list, consider what it was that motivated you to act in the face of fear. What was it that compelled you to move forward, even though you were afraid? Was it the thought that pushing through the fear would result in a much better outcome than the current situation? Was it in the service of something or someone other than yourself? If someone else, who was it? Was it for the rescue or protection of yourself or someone else? If someone else, who? Was it that you felt strongly that something needed to be done and no one else would or could do what you did? Was it simply the right thing to do? Are there patterns to your courageousness? Do you tend to be more courageous when the well-being of others is at stake? Or how about when you see an injustice being done?

You discover your values through this exercise. Paying attention to your courageous acts will tell you what you're about.

I reviewed my own list of courageous acts and realized that my courage seemed to be primarily triggered by two things:

① the hope and desire of something *better* for myself and/or my family; or

② an innate calling that something *needed* to be done about a situation or incident.

Now that you've examined your own courageous acts, you can employ this knowledge of yourself and your values to further develop your courage. The next time you feel fear, answer the following questions:

a) What is the greatest potential outcome of moving forward (through the fear)?

b) What's the worst-case scenario if I do nothing?

c) Is the potential best-case scenario (a) worth risking the worst-case scenario (b)? Or in other words—given my values (what's important to me), am I willing to miss out on (a) in order to avoid experiencing (b)?

In this way, your decision to act, or not, will come from a place of calm, cool reasoning, from a place of COURAGEOUS FEMININITY.

Femininity

Whoa! Back up. Did I just use the words *courageous* and *femininity* in the same sentence? Yes, I did.

Be honest—does the word femininity make you cringe a little? Is your instinctive reaction to think *weak* or *manipulative, helpless, passive* or *submissive?* Do the words *courage* and *feminine* seem like they don't go together? Do you envision a 1950's laundry detergent ad of a housewife wearing full makeup, a dress, and high-heeled pumps while vacuuming the living room? Do you think of frilly curtains and pink teddy bears? Do you think of a quiet, polite, pretty woman being completely ignored in a boardroom?

I'd like to challenge you that these ideas, taken all together, are a stereotypical *exaggeration* of femininity. It's time to take this word back and to embrace what we as women bring to the world.

Early in my adulthood, I was a single parent at home and a rarity in male-dominated organizations at work. At home, I was nurturer and disciplinarian, cook and mechanic, breadwinner and bill payer. I kept up the house and maintained the lawn. At work, I managed teams of people and large projects in technical divisions staffed predominantly with former military men.

In both environments—home and work—it was helpful and easy to adopt qualities like bravado, fierce independence, and a 'show no weakness' mentality. These behaviors are an *exaggeration of masculinity;* as surely as helplessness is an exaggeration of femininity. These affectations certainly helped me get ahead in my career. Today, I'm aware that by downplaying some of my natural qualities, I diminished my contribution. I wasn't playing 'full out.'

Anything inauthentic becomes an energy drain eventually, and this showed up dramatically in my relationships. If you've ever tried to maintain any kind of relationship, romantic or otherwise, while holding on to a 'show no weakness' attitude, you know exactly what I mean.

Many of us have stifled aspects of our femininity in order to thrive in certain environments. We avoid asking for help because we don't want to appear incompetent. We avoid showing compassion because we don't want to look soft. We avoid sharing a contrary opinion because we don't want to appear 'bitchy.' And yet, collaboration, thoughtfulness, and an opinion based on our own experience might be the very things that are needed in the situation.

Do we really want to discourage so many of our human qualities from entering our workplaces, governments, courtrooms, and boardrooms? Or is it just possible that by ignoring or underestimating the natural gifts of half the human population that we're missing out on some real solutions to some real problems we face today in our world?

Maybe it's time to recognize that our homes aren't the only places that can benefit from a feminine touch.

> *"Promoting feminine leadership traits is less an issue of male vs. female, but a question of whether we are over-looking qualities that may be crucial to navigating 21st century business challenges."*
> *Janet Crawford*

For every force of nature, there is an equal but opposite force. And each force has its uses in getting things done. So while we embrace our independence, let's not forget the value of collaboration. While we honor knowledge and reason, let's equally honor intuition. While we move forward assertively tackling problems, let's do it with grace and with empathy both for those who will immediately benefit, as well as those who will initially feel unsettled by the change.

A Healthy Dose of Good Trouble

So let me ask you: when was the last time you *looked like trouble?* The kind of trouble that excites? The kind that holds the promise of better things to come? The kind that signifies a turning point, a twist of fate, a fulfillment of your destiny? When was the last time you got that look in your eye that said you were going to break down some barriers and nothing could stop you? Would there ever be a better time to do that than right now?

Explore and discover the depths of your heart. Acknowledge and own what you're willing to fight for, what's important enough that you'll move forward even when you're afraid. Show up as the *true, authentic, whole being that you are* beneath your fears and doubts. Consider that what the world has been missing is *you*, and stop denying the world your gifts. If you do all of that, I promise you're going to look more and more like trouble to those around you.

I can't wait to see who you inspire with your crazy-brave authentic self!

Go start some trouble!

Success Strategies

1. Breaking through barriers, stepping outside of your comfort zone, and *fulfilling your destiny* will bring on an exhilarating mixture of vulnerability and determination, confidence and humility, fear and courage.

2. Becoming *truly authentic* and showing up in the world as the real you takes courage and may be the biggest challenge you face in life.

3. Examining your *courageous acts* will help you discover your values.

4. It's time to *embrace* and *celebrate* what we as women bring to the world.

5. Consider that what the world has been missing is YOU, and *go start some trouble!*

Notes

Lotte Vesterli

Lotte is an Occupational Therapist, Certified Coach, Master RIM-facilitator, and Founder of Vesterli Coaching. She works with people who have suffered all kinds of traumatic experiences—from childhood bullying to domestic violence and sexual abuse.

She is author of *Life after Bullying: A Three-step Process to Inner Peace.* Her extensive toolbox includes Jack Canfield's *Train the Trainer,* Dr. Deborah Sandella's RIM method, and Chunyi Lin's Spring Forest Qigong.

Lotte can help you surface and discharge negative emotions so that you live life to the fullest and achieve your dreams.

www.lotte@vesterli.com
www.lifeafterbullying.com

SECTION 3: CHAPTER 4

Intuition – The Secret Tool for Success

by Lotte Vesterli

> *"What I am looking for is not out there. It is in me."*
> *Helen Keller*

Trusting Your Intuition

I had gone to the airport to pick up my husband, who was returning from a business trip to France. I couldn't wait to see him again, especially because I had something very exciting to tell him when we got home.

As we met, my husband shared with me that he had unsuccessfully tried to send me flowers during Wednesday's lunch break. This was totally unexpected and unusual. By now I could hardly wait to get home! Not only did I have big news to share, I had also just gotten a huge insight into how powerful our intuition is.

Wednesday during my lunch break, I was sitting at the doctor's office getting the news that I was pregnant with our first child!

We are all born with strong intuition. As we grow older, our teachers and other adults often tell us only to trust direct knowledge and facts—not the things we intuitively know but can't explain. Relearning to trust your intuition will open you to gain insight and act on inspiration. It will help you move forward with more ease and speed. As you get more in tune with your intuition, your ability to connect with and support other people expands.

Since that day I have been on a journey developing my intuition. I will share some of the transformational tools I am using throughout this chapter. Today I know that we intuitively get ideas about which questions to ask and which tools to use—both externally and internally—if we just listen within ourselves. I use this knowledge today with great results in my coaching business as well as in my own ongoing development.

You, too, can develop your intuition to use for your personal and career benefit. When you develop your intuition and tune in to your coworkers, students, clients, or customers, you understand them in a deeper way. This allows you to help them grow in the way they deserve.

> *"A woman uses her intelligence to find reasons to support her intuition."* Gilbert K. Chesterton

Developing your intuition—an inner sense of knowing—is a proven way to move forward towards your success. Learning to listen within will help you maintain balance and well-being. For me, learning to trust my intuition has helped me connect with new people, trust myself more, increase my self-esteem, and live a life aligned with my purpose.

There are many ways to develop your intuition. All personal development is really about giving you a deeper awareness of your inner self and allowing your intuition to flow. One of the great methods I have been using for the past 20 years is meditation. Download a free guided meditation at *www.lifeafterbullying.com/downloadsuw.*

Meditations open you up for your intuitive voice to come forward into your conscious awareness. Any form of meditation works, including quiet walks in nature and sitting relaxed, focusing on something calming. When you meditate, quiet your mind as best you can in the moment. Don't worry about your inner chatter, accept it in the moment. You might imagine it floating away on a white fluffy cloud, knowing that important thoughts get back to you when the time is right. Through quieting your mind, you will let go of stress. Over time, you become more in tune with yourself, your feelings, and inner inspiration.

When you have finished your meditation, you might have gained some insight and inspiration that you are not consciously aware of. You may now choose to write in your journal, while sitting peacefully. Write down any word that comes to mind without thinking too much. Keep writing as long as you have words coming to you. At the end of the journaling, read through what you have written and underline the important things you want to remember.

Meditation, journaling and developing my intuition are the three tools that have helped me in my life—perhaps they will help you as well.

Open up by forgiving the past

Do you have a hard time achieving success in your business or life in general? That may be caused by inner beliefs and emotions that consciously or subconsciously hold you back. When you have experienced a traumatic situation of any kind in your life, it often sticks with you until you work on it. In this case you might experience difficulties with trusting yourself and others. In the past, I worked with my own feelings of low self-esteem and a belief that I was not good enough and not worthy of success.

Luckily, you can change both your conscious and the even more important subconscious beliefs.

To create success, it is important that you stay true to yourself and live according to your own values. This requires you to consciously work on your inner beliefs and *let go of the past*. That will allow you to start being in tune with yourself and the people you work with. You don't have to be perfect, but you have to start the process and keep moving forward. This will open you to experience a deeper level of empathy and compassion towards yourself and others.

For many years, I held onto my past, blaming my negative experiences for making me a person with low self-esteem, self-worth, or self-love. My first three years of school were a nightmare. My teacher treated me as though I were unable to learn. She treated me like a slow learner, and my classmates followed up on this. I wasn't invited to any parties, didn't have friends, and was never included in any games.

As a result, at the end of third grade, I couldn't read or write. I had lost any positive belief I might have had about myself. I had almost lost my voice: it had grown quiet and barely audible. I would eat for comfort and sit in my tree as a way of escaping the world.

My recovery journey was long. At times I moved three steps forward and two steps back. You can read about my journey in my book *Life after Bullying: A Three-step Process to Inner Peace.*

One of the big steps forward in my recovery was when I learned what forgiving was all about. I always felt that if I forgave, I would give power to the bullies. I would tell them that it was okay that they robbed me of my childhood and my self-esteem. One day I realized that when we forgive, we are opening up our soul. We regain our own power by releasing the past.

Forgiving is not about giving in or stating that it is okay to hurt other people. Forgiving is about *letting go so new inspiration can flow through you.*

The person who is able to forgive is strong like Nelson Mandela. He was imprisoned for 27 years and was still able to forgive his captors. After his release, he defeated apartheid, and served as a true inspiration for millions around the world.

Think of forgiving in this way: have you ever done anything wrong in your life? Or said something hurtful to another person? Unless you are a saint, you probably have. You might also have forgotten most of what you have said or done. Most of the times we say or do something, we do it without realizing that it can hurt other people. The fact is that our response to something is affected by our past experiences. This means that everyone will respond and act differently in any situation.

Today I no longer believe that my teacher and classmates hurt me on purpose. I am sure that they weren't consciously aware of what they did to me. This realization made it easier for me to forgive. I have also realized that by holding on to my past, I created a shield and was using considerable energy to hold it in place. By forgiving, I experienced freedom and inner peace. I am feeling more powerful in a good way and have more energy. Most importantly, today I truly believe that I am good enough. I believe that I can achieve what I want and I feel compassion towards myself and other people.

I encourage you to forgive your past. You will feel stronger, more empowered, and more open to try out new things. You will also open up so your intuition can flow. What does your ideal life look like? Who do you need to forgive in order to move a step closer towards this life? Write it down.

One person that we often forget to forgive is ourself! Are you having thoughts like, "I wish I had...," "If only I...," or "Why can't I...?" Release and forgive yourself. Know that you have done the best you possibly could until now with the awareness and knowledge you have gained so far.

Accessing your creative mind

Going though life, we experience what I call 'Life Lessons.' These life lessons are designed to help us learn new things and to become consciously aware of what we already know.

One weekend I volunteered to be in charge of planning and providing meals for about one hundred young adults, making sure that their energy level was up for optimal learning. Volunteering was quite a bit of work. Sometimes I had to move fast and didn't get much sleep yet still had fun.

When I told people about my weekend experience, they looked at me as though I were crazy, and asked me questions like "How on earth could you do that?" "How did you know how much food to make?" and "How did you organize that?" At first, I didn't think much about these comments. As I continued receiving these responses, I decided to take a deeper look into what I had done. I realized that for me it wasn't a big deal to cook a meal for a hundred people when I had extra hands available to help.

When discovering our inner resources, it is important to ask the following two questions:

What insight can I gain from this experience/task?

Taking a deeper look at the experience made me realize several talents that came naturally to me: like planning, organizing, guiding people, being open minded, and capable of finding solutions in every situation.

 Where in my life am I, or could I be, using these qualities?

Answering this question gave me valuable insights: a deeper knowledge about how I could make positive changes, both in my personal life and my work.

These two questions are important to help us gain insight into our own abilities. Ask yourself these questions whenever you have done something significant. Answer the questions from both a professional and personal view to learn the most about yourself. I continue to ask myself these questions whenever I sense I can get a deeper awareness of my own abilities.

These questions will help you extract your insight and learn about yourself and your unique toolbox.

When things happen in life, we often act *automatically* without being aware of what we are doing. The reality is that the life lessons we have learned from our past experiences provide us with the inner strength that we use today.

Think about why you bought this book. You probably wanted to change your situation and move forward in your life. To move forward, you need to get in tune with what your toolbox looks like today. This toolbox contains both the things you have learned, the good or bad experience you have had, and the skills you have gained over time.

Be aware that not all the tools we possess are appropriate. Getting to know your toolbox gives you conscious access to the tools so you have the ability to make changes. As you become aware of your tools, you can start playing with them. Be creative and combine them in ways that fit your need in the current moment.

My experience is that one tool might work great to help me move forward in one situation and a combination of other tools helps with something else. As you become more aware of your tools, you will also notice the tools that aren't working to support you. This can be a spontaneous reaction or a habit. Ask yourself: "What would be a better solution?" and start implementing this. Over time, you will be able to substitute old tools with new tools that work better for you.

As you open up to your intuition, you will become more aware of your strengths and inner knowledge. You will gain more creativity in your solutions and your intuition will guide you to spontaneously choose the right tool at the right moment.

Moving forward, I encourage you to keep working on yourself and keep noticing the changes that happen!

Success Strategies

1. *Meditate* on a regular basis.

2. *Forgive* yourself and others.

3. Access your *creative mind.*

4. Open up your own *greatness* by uncovering your unique toolbox.

5. Do these exercises on a regular basis and notice what *changes* occur.

6. Keep a diary where you record your *positive experiences.*

Jennie Ritchie

Jennie is a celebrated teacher, speaker and writer. She received her BA degree in Math/Dance Education from Brigham Young University in 1992.

She has taught middle and high school for 20 years in California and Utah. Jennie is active in her church and has spoken to youth and womens' groups nationwide on topics such as self-esteem, goal-setting, and overcoming challenges.

She is the author of the acclaimed book *Keeping It Together When Life Throws You Curves, a Major League Wife's Guide to Overcoming Challenges with Faith and Fortitude.*

Jennie is married and currently resides with her husband, Wally, and their three children in St. George, Utah, where she teaches middle school.

www.jennieritchie.com

SECTION 3: CHAPTER 5

Stick-to-it-iveness

by Jennie Ritchie

> *"We can do anything we want as long as we stick to it long enough."* Helen Keller

When I was 5 years old, we lived on a quiet cul-de-sac in sunny, Southern California. There were lots of kids in our neighborhood. Since those were the days before electronic devices, most afternoons my sister and I could be found riding bikes and playing in the street. One summer day, we were playing outside and Pam, an older girl, offered me a ride behind her on the bike. What an honor! I hopped on and away we went, my legs dangling freely below the seat.

By the time my screams registered with her, the damage had been done. My right heel had become caught in the spokes of the rear tire, and as it turned, it ripped through the skin and tendon…all the way to the bone. My parents were horrified when they came upon me lying in the street, and they rushed me to the hospital. My mom thought I'd never walk again, or at least not without permanent damage. The doctors bound the wound with a special dressing that had to be changed morning and night. Because the dressing stuck to the wound, I had to soak it in a hot bath twice a day in order for my parents to remove it. It was excruciatingly painful. And so began the six-month process of healing and learning to walk again.

After a period of time, we started exercises to help me learn to put my heel down. In order to do that, I had to stretch the damaged tendon. I can distinctly remember standing at the top of the stairs, holding onto the railing and crying out in pain while we practiced pressing my heel to the ground. It was incredibly painful and I know I wanted to give up more than once. Thankfully, I didn't give up, and, over time, I was able to walk, run, bike, dance, and swim without any long-lasting damage. With the help of my parents, I was able to overcome that challenge because I didn't give up. I still have a nasty scar on my heel and it serves as a reminder that I can emerge successful when I stay focused on the goal.

Stick to the Task

People quit things every day—they quit jobs, school, relationships, churches, social groups, and many other ventures. In my life and in my career as a teacher, I've seen many people quit before a task was complete, before a goal was reached, before success was achieved. Why?

There are many reasons people don't follow through on their visions and goals. But if we want the success that is waiting for us, we're going to have to stick to the task. My definition of 'stick-to-it-iveness' is the ability to accomplish one's goal even though the journey is difficult or unpleasant. My success in life has come in large part due to my ability to stick to a goal, grin and bear it, and stay committed to my family on our journey down this road called Life. I got married to a professional baseball player when I was 18 years old. I've moved our family all over the country, had trouble getting pregnant, at times provided the sole financial support for our family, and the list goes on. What's my secret? Grin & Bear It. And if you don't feel like grinning, fake it. Sometimes we have to put our head down, put a smile on our face, and stick to the task. This will bring you the success you seek.

My husband, Wally, was a major league baseball player—a left-handed relief pitcher for the Philadelphia Phillies. Besides playing in the major leagues, he pitched for many minor league teams across the country. Change was a constant in our lives. In 1994 he got a job playing with the Detroit Tigers AAA team in Toledo, Ohio. Since I had to finish my teaching contract each year before joining him for the summer, I ended up driving cross-country with either my mom or my sister as co-pilot.

That year would be different. After being married for nearly six years, we had finally become pregnant. I was three months along when my mom and I packed our car to the gills, including our dog, and set out on our 2,000-mile, cross-country drive.

If you've ever set out on a long road trip like this, you know you can't count each mile. You can't focus on each pothole or construction delay. If you do, the obstacles will look overwhelming and reaching your goal will seem impossible. You are headed for your destination and that's all that matters. We couldn't focus on the fact that we were only in Denver or Kansas City. Similarly, you can't focus on the roadblocks in your path or how much further you have to go. You have to keep your eyes on where you want to end up.

Keep Your Eyes on the Destination

When we are on the road to success, we need to keep our eyes on the destination, even if it seems like only a teeny dot in the distance. I have taught a variety of students from 7th through 12th grade, and, unfortunately, many are short-sighted—they only focus on what is in front of them. If they have social plans, or drama arises, that takes precedence over their schoolwork. Many students I've taught over the years have unlimited potential, but when the task seems too difficult, they choose the road that seems easiest at the moment. Instead of keeping their eyes on the success destination, they only look as far as Friday night.

Does that sound like us? Of course! We're human. But if we want to achieve the success that is waiting, we must stick to the task...whether the potholes on our road to success are financial issues, relationship struggles, or other temporary detours, we have to keep our eyes on the destination. We can't focus on the bumps; we have to focus on where we're headed.

Here's an exercise that has helped me, and I know it will work for you. Find a quiet place and choose one goal that represents success for you. A *Success Destination,* if you will. Now, identify three challenges that are either already visible or may appear as you head toward that destination.

Next, imagine yourself achieving that goal (getting that promotion, graduating from college, achieving financial success...) by painting a picture in your head. In your mind's eye, see where you are standing or sitting, who is around you, what you are doing, what emotions you are feeling, and so on. Spend some time enjoying your success, celebrating the accomplishment. Make your picture as vivid as you possibly can, and each time you go through this exercise, increase the detail of the picture in your mind.

Lastly, from where you are standing—at the success destination—look back to see the challenges you identified earlier. They won't look the same. I assure you that they will look smaller and more surmountable. Repeat this exercise at least daily—or as often as you need the strength to stick to your drive toward your success destination.

Wally and I were living in Southern California in 2004. We had returned to the Golden State in 1998 to continue Wally's baseball career and remained there when his career ended, so he could complete his education. We loved the area, but for many reasons decided that we needed to leave California to raise our family somewhere with a slower pace of life. Our two older children were nine and seven years old and our baby girl was 1½ at the time. I struggled with symptoms of depression after she was born but was still managing to teach high school part-time and hold our house together.

In the process of relocating, my husband looked outside of California for work and had gone through the interview process with a company in Arizona. Summer was coming, our lease was ending shortly, and we still hadn't received word about the job. Recognizing that we needed to move our family, but not knowing for sure where, we took a big risk and packed up everything we owned into portable storage units. Next, we loaded our clothing, baby items, irreplaceable photo albums, important documents, and the kids into our two vehicles and moved in with family members. We were temporarily jobless and homeless.

After 10 days without news, we headed to Northern Utah to attend a Labor Day family reunion. During his weeks of job hunting, Wally had put several "feelers" out to friends throughout the west, including the town of St. George, Utah, where we used to live. Our family and friends thought we were crazy to have left our home without a secure job and no idea where we would end up.

While at the family reunion, Wally found out through a friend of a friend, that there was a job opening in St. George, and that he had been recommended for it. Wally interviewed on our return from the reunion and was offered the position. We returned to California to pick up our other car, then headed back to Utah to begin our life there. Over the years, we have grown to love our new home, our children have flourished, and we have connected as a family. In hindsight, it was a scary process, but definitely the best decision for our family's well-being.

Be True to Yourself

Wally and I had a common vision of what was best for our family and it was leaving California. We had to be true to that vision. It didn't matter how bizarre it seemed or what other people thought. You may have had similar experiences. Have you had moments when you were being ridiculed for sticking to your success goals? It doesn't matter how crazy it seems to you or to other people looking in from the outside. You have to be true to your own visions and goals. The power of stick-to-it-iveness will keep you heading toward your vision of success. Be true to yourself and your vision. You will make it.

I didn't teach school for the first couple years after we moved to Utah. However, when my youngest was four, I needed to return to work to help support the family. I graduated from college in Math and Dance Education and had always taught high school classes in those areas. A middle school teaching job came up very close to our home and seemed like an ideal fit. The only hitch was that it included teaching business courses, such as keyboarding, marketing, and a computer tech course. Although I had taught for almost 10 years at that point, I had never taught technology classes before and especially in middle school (yikes!). It wasn't the original plan, but we decided it was the right decision at the time.

As a condition of employment, I needed to complete courses before I started teaching and then take additional courses while teaching until my certification was complete. It was mountains of extra work and it definitely wasn't a comfortable transition for me, but I had to believe I could do it successfully—and I did. I taught middle school business courses for the next six years and really enjoyed it. Sometimes plans change—and often it's not comfortable—but we can be successful if we stick to our goals and believe in ourselves.

Believe You Can

In order to be successful, we need to believe or at least have a spark of hope that we can succeed. Without that firm belief, we won't be able to stick to our vision when the roadblocks appear. Plans may need to be adjusted. The path may be uncomfortable and wind through uncharted territory, as my business teaching did. Don't let that deter you. Gain every skill you can along the way, because you never know which one you'll need around the next bend. For example, I became a fast typist, and it turned out to be a benefit when I needed to teach Keyboarding classes.

Research the best routes, make smart decisions, modify the plan as needed, and then stick to it. When we believe in ourselves, success is inevitable.

Our home is very close to the incredible beauty of Zion National Park. We love to visit and enjoy a variety of day hikes. One of the available hikes is called Observation Point, an eight-hour round-trip hike with an elevation change of 2,100 feet. As evidenced in many online photos, those who have made it to the top, find the 360° views breathtaking.

My husband is a much stronger hiker than I and was eager to give it a shot. Let's say I was...less than eager. He motivated me by saying that we could turn back if the hike became too difficult. It wasn't very strenuous in the beginning and I thought to myself, "this isn't going to be bad at all," but that didn't last long. The hike was difficult, to say the least. Many sections of the trail were steep and occasionally there was only a thin ledge overlooking a devastating drop. I tried to keep thinking of the beautiful views at the top and how good I would feel about myself when I made it.

My knees hurt, my back ached, and I felt like I couldn't go another step. I seriously considered turning back more than once. At these times, I somehow managed to put my head down and push on. I knew I had to stick to it. When we reached the summit, it was all worth it. It was incredibly gorgeous and, even though it was merely a hike to some people, it was a major success for me.

Your Reward Awaits

Often, when we start on our road to success, we don't know exactly what we'll face. The path may start out flat and easy, but at some point you're going to have to make an uphill climb. We know success is waiting for us at the top, but there are times when we want to give up. Don't. Don't ever give up. Keep pushing through and sticking to the goal you've set. Success comes after the struggle. Visualize the amazing view, and then make it happen. Your reward is waiting for you at the top.

Congratulations. You made it!

Success Strategies

1. *Keep your success goals in mind.* As needed, practice the Success Destination exercise described in this chapter.

2. *Be true to yourself and your vision,* no matter what others say.

3. *Consistently build your belief in yourself.* You are your biggest support.

4. No matter what comes along, *push through* when challenges arise.

5. *Stick-to-it-iveness* is key to achieving the success you desire.

Carla White

Carla engages, entertains, and empowers women to build healthy, resilient, and inspired lives. Through her keynotes and workshops she shares humorous stories, positive energy, and practical tips to help her audiences connect to happiness. She is a champion for change and courageous living.

Carla started her career as a nurse over 20 years ago. Searching for adventure and challenge, she became a Fire Fighter and Emergency Response Professional.

She started Crisp Connections Inc. in 2013 and provides presentations for teams and businesses on employee engagement and team building.

Carla is author of ***Showing Up – Lessons in Happiness, Humour and the Courageous Heart.***

www.CrispConnections.ca
www.Carla-White.ca

SECTION 3: CHAPTER 6

What's So Funny About Success?

by Carla White

> *"I love people who make me laugh. I honestly think it's the thing I like most, to laugh. It cures a multitude of ills. It's probably the most important thing in a person." Audrey Hepburn*

When I was asked to be a part of this incredible group of women writing about success, I was humbled, I was honoured...and I was horrified! I wondered how I had fooled them into thinking I was a success. After all, I drive a second-hand Ford Explorer named Ruby; I'm not even close to my goal weight; and just last week I did a three-hour workshop where, two minutes in, my control top pantyhose retreated to rest around my upper thighs! The triumph was that the audience didn't notice; at least I don't think they did.

Then, to top it off, the editors wanted this chapter to be funny. They were asking an academic, high-achieving, up-tight perfectionist to write about how humour helped me on the road to success. Simple—I stumbled onto it!

Humour in Hindsight

I remember one night when I had a deadline at work (the boss was demanding I deal with a cranky client) and my daughter had just thrown up on the dog for the third time when my husband, Stew, breezed through the door to ask, "What's for supper?" He didn't even see the phone flying at his head when I screamed, "Take-out." The irony is that those chaotic, stress-filled, crap-raining-down-on-your-day kind of moments are when we could most use a sense of humour, but in reality we are looking for the first upright thing to punch in the face. Any utterances from me during those times were generally profane shrieks that sent the kids scattering, the dog hiding in the kennel, and my husband trying to get in beside him.

It is in retrospect that I am able to find the funny in my life. While I am going through often ridiculous and chaotic experiences, the only laughter that may emerge is a hysterical high-pitched cackle that has even me questioning my sanity. Afterwards, when I am privately processing, or telling someone the story, that is when I see the comedic value. It's taken me years to get to this practice.

There was a long period in my life when I wasn't able to do that. For ten years I was treated for depression. There wasn't much I laughed about, and I certainly didn't see the humour in my situation.

When my daughter, Sianna, was born, I chose to be a stay-at-home mom. Two-and-a-half years later, I had the twins, Rylee and Shaelyn. Obviously, I had a ton of time on my hands to enjoy life! While it's true that I was busy with three little ones, it was the overwhelming sadness, irritation, and apathy that kept me in a perpetual downward spiral. I didn't feel like doing anything fun, and the less time I spent enjoying myself, the more reasons I had to not laugh and enjoy life. The antidepressants kept my emotions flat—I had no lows, but no highs, either. My sense of 'ha-ha' was more like 'bla-bla.'

Then, at a pivotal moment while watching my kids play in our backyard, I decided that the way I was existing was definitely not the legacy I wanted to leave for them. With the help of my doctor, I weaned myself off the antidepressants and slowly began to feel more emotion—the good, the bad, and the ugly.

What surprised me most was that, as I started to process emotions and work through issues, I got my sense of humour back. It wasn't like I received a package in the mail and there it was. Little by little, I saw things in a different light. I started looking for opportunities to laugh. Sometimes it was a little forced, but it always made me feel better. Soon, the giddy, goofy girl from the farm emerged again. Now I use humour and positive thinking to keep from going back to the darkness of depression. Seeing the lighter side of life and not taking myself so seriously gets me through stressful and difficult situations—like dropping my drawers in front of a group of 60 workshop participants. It helps me to be more productive and, even better, humour connects me with people.

Climbing the Ladder of Success

I had a personal trainer who introduced me to the Jacob's Ladder™ cardio machine, with continuous bars on a 45-degree angle that moved as I climbed. It should have been called the Crush-Carla's-Spirit Ladder—no matter how many times I pulled my exhausted body up to the next level, one more rung would appear, and I never reached the top. I felt like a hamster, just more sweaty and frustrated. The trainer, the ladder, and I have all parted ways. For a long time, that was how I saw the climb to success.

I was no stranger to hard work. I watched others around me do it constantly. Growing up on the farm, watching my parents toil daily to make a living, I bought into the idea that in order to get ahead you had to put your nose to the grindstone, that life was hard, and that struggles built character. This was the solemn determination that fuelled the start of my business. It wasn't much fun.

Lurking in the back of my mind was what every executive mom starting her own business wants: copious amounts of wine, a good-looking male assistant, and chocolate. Since none of those was likely to provide an income, I needed to look somewhere else. So I set about getting clarity on what success meant for me.

For many, success is easy to define by metrics of money, belongings, or job status. However, my barometer was laughter. I want my business to be a reflection of me and my personality— someone who loves to laugh and help others feel better.

How Humour Helps

I have joked during a particularly harsh performance review, talked an angry store clerk down from a career-ending rant, and even laughed out loud at a funeral. In the moments when emotions are escalated, or tension and stress are getting the best of us, laughter takes the pressure off.

And, again, it wasn't always this way for me.

At a weekend scrapbooking event, allowing my inner perfectionist to take charge, I had toiled over the placement of each picture and struggled with every aspect of page layouts. I fretted about not getting anything done, and the frustration and tension escalated. The pressure manifested as a squeezing tightness in my chest. Suddenly, like the pop of a champagne cork, the tension released itself in the form of a giddy, effervescent giggle.

Wait. Maybe that's a bit too gracious a description. It was more like an overly dramatic, completely goofy chortle as I threw myself on the table to express my dismay. The outburst was enough to startle my tablemates and someone laughed. Pretty soon the four of us at the table were hooting and squealing as tears rolled down our faces.

The three conference organizers left their seats to join in the festivities. As the fits of laughter died down, someone would suck in air or snort, and set us off on another gale of guffaws. None of us cared that we were drawing attention to our corner of the room, and a few more ladies approached to share in the laughter.

The merriment went on for about a half hour before things settled down and we all turned our attention back to our scrapbooking. As I looked down at my page, I was suddenly struck by an inspiration. I smiled to myself as I easily created the design, which later won a contest. It is one of the best I have ever produced, thanks to a moment where I let go and laughed, finding the humour in the moment.

We've all heard that exercise releases endorphins and other feel-good hormones. Well, so does laughter, and I would much rather have aches from side-splitting laughter than from going to the gym anytime. (Remember, this is because I suffer from post-traumatic ladder disorder.)

Research supports the multitude of benefits that laughter and a sense of humour have on performance. When something makes us smile or laugh, a rush of dopamine is released into our systems. This feel-good hormone activates the learning centers in the brain and heightens creativity, productivity, and engagement.

In an article in Forbes® titled, *Are Funny People More Successful in Business?* the former president of the Association for Applied and Therapeutic Humor, Steven Sultanoff, PhD., stated, "If someone is using humor, then they are connecting with people and building relationships, which creates opportunities that others may not have." I definitely used my wit to bond with others. People who make me laugh energize me. I have received many client referrals and built my business because of my ability to connect in a positive way.

Recently, I was in for a routine dental check-up and my hygienist, Cheryl, informed me that my dentist of 20 years was no longer at the practice so I would have a new guy checking my teeth. As he examined my pearly whites, he commented, "The last patient jumped out of the chair 'cause my hands were so cold."

I looked him right in the eye and, talking around the dental instruments he had just put in my mouth, I mumbled, "It's a good thing you weren't doing a prostate exam!"

Dr. Tony and Cheryl burst out laughing, and I knew that I had connected with my new dentist. As I was leaving the office, Cheryl was still chuckling and said, "He'll be using that joke all day now."

Judy Carter, internationally acclaimed humourist and communications expert, says, "It isn't your credentials that make you unique and memorable, but it's sharing your own 'Mess-to-Success' journey." I had messes all right, but who doesn't?

The fact is we all have our struggles and challenges. The difference is whether we pack them in a suitcase and carry them with us everywhere or hang them on the line and let the neighbours see our underwear. By making the choice to not take myself so seriously and sharing my baggage with people in a funny way, my life is a lot more enjoyable. Without realizing or planning for it, I have stumbled on a new career as an amateur humourist.

Stand Up Success

As I stood on the stage sipping from my giant wine glass, quipping about life in the "White" house, I revelled in the laughter from the audience and the woman who kept talking out loud in response to my jokes. She wasn't heckling me, just encouraging me as she related to the amusing scenarios. I was one of six people who volunteered to perform a stand-up comedy act about our struggles with mental illness in a *Stand-Up for Mental Health* show. I had been asked by one of the organizers to participate.

Janine knew about my previous battle with depression, but her comment, "We want you 'cause we think you're hilarious," totally fed my diva ego! Coming up with the material was easy: I used my life experiences as an angry housewife turned executive mom with three kids, a dog, and a husband.

I had gone from the depths of depression, full of rage, to a recovering perfectionist able to turn my messes into a successful stand-up routine. All those years in high school as a goofy class clown doing the occasional imitation of Mrs. Haviggins from *The Carol Burnett Show* culminated in that moment as I stood center stage and heard people laugh. I got my first standing ovation!

Later, my husband admitted that I am funny and do have a sense of humour. Now, *that's* success!

Humour Habits

My perfectionism, negative thinking, and limiting beliefs certainly contributed to my plunge into depression. During the sad times, I did still have moments of levity, but my sense of humour was more caustic and self-deprecating and it had a really whiny tone to it. I have such a long-standing, close personal relationship with my inner critic that it was really a challenge to kick her to the curb.

And if my ex-psychiatrist is reading this, I do not have multiple personality disorder. I have worked to turn my inner chatter into inner chuckles. A really helpful exercise for me was to write down all the stories of my life—the good, the bad and the crazy—and then review them to see how they were funny. Not all of them were. But with the passage of time, and a change in attitude, I definitely have some material that keeps me in a positive mindset—and perhaps back to the stage with another comedy act.

During the depths of my despair, my husband used to tell me, "Just choose to be happy." I wanted to punch him in the face. That was something I had to work on, so I didn't add an even bigger mess to my already full plate.

Laughter helped me. Now I'm able to stay in the moment so I make a conscious decision to look for laugh-out-loud moments. When it's -30 degrees Celsius outside, my dog cocks his leg inside and does a three-legged hop out to pee, it cracks me up every time! I have a humour file on my laptop where I keep cartoons, jokes, and YouTube™ videos that make me laugh. Watching clips from *The Carol Burnett Show* or episodes of *Mrs. Brown's Boys* never disappoints when I am feeling the need for cheerfulness.

Most importantly, I've dropped out of the snitch-and-bitch club, also known as coffee with the girls. I observed that I have boundless energy when I surround myself with people who make me laugh. My *Success University for Women*™ co-author and soul sister, Danne Reed, helps me see the obscure, ridiculous, and hilarious in my life when I am standing knee-deep in the muck. My sense of humour and the ability to laugh at myself helps me cope with the stresses of running a business and managing a family—without frequent trips to the psychiatrist's office. I love that my funny stories help those around me as well.

I am reminded of Maya Angelou's famous quote, "I've learned that people will forget what you said, people will forget what you did, but people will never forget how you made them feel."

Giving other people the opportunity to have fun and enjoy life is something I am passionate about and it increases my happiness. I once had a woman approach me at a social event to tell me that she had been in one of my workshops two years earlier and had learned so much because of the hilarious stories I shared to illustrate the learning points.

That's the legacy I want to leave...one of humour, happiness, and connection.

Success Strategies

1. *Smile.* It is only a small leap from a smile to a laugh.

2. *Find humour in the craziness of a busy life.* Look for laugh-out-loud moments or create them by watching sitcoms, reading funny books, or looking at cartoons. Watch your pets and children!

3. Hang out with people who *make you laugh* or *laugh with you.*

4. Let go—and LAUGH.

Section 4

Soaring in Success

SECTION 4: INTRODUCTION

*O*nce upon a time, a little girl worked hard only once in a while, never had anything go wrong, and achieved success with no effort at all. But here in the real world, we know that's a fallacy—mostly. Some of us cling to the hope that if we work hard enough, long enough, eventually it will get easier, right? Well, sometimes, but more often than not, success takes stamina, constant evolving, learning to dance through life with grace and courage, and staying connected to the true source of wisdom.

The authors you are about to read in *Soaring in Success* learned to do just that. ***Success University for Women***™ Co-Founder *Jan Fraser* of the USA and Bermuda exemplifies Unsinkability in so many ways. Dubai's *Carol Talbot* became a life-long student and now teaches others to get out of their own way. American *Amina Makhdoom* shows by example the benefits of Ease and Flow versus forcing and striving toward success.

Jacqueline Throop-Robinson shares how her Passion for her business propelled her toward success, while American *J.L. (Jani) Ashmore* bravely teaches us to be Fearless on the road to success. And last but by no means least, *Dr. Anita Sanchez* of the USA shows us how connection to her ancestors and Spirit guides her on life's journey.

From Dubai to Bermuda, and many points in between, these women all encountered similar challenges and learned how to overcome them to *soar* in their success. May you gain their wisdom and courage as they share their hearts and stories with you.

Jan Fraser

Jan is the definition of a 'self-starter,' bringing real world experience to her keynotes, training, and coaching. An airline industry superstar, she rose from the ramp support team to the ticket counter to flight attendant to instructor, training more than 20,000 flight attendants.

Her engaging style, sparkling humor, and extra-mile attitude have made her a much-loved motivator and coach. Jan has conducted training for Fortune 500 companies, small businesses, schools, colleges, women's organizations, library systems, prisons, and associations.

She has trained with and assists *Chicken Soup for the Soul*® author Jack Canfield with his hugely popular self-esteem and success seminars. Jan is the author of three books: *Ordinary Women...Extraordinary Success; Keeping Customers for Life;* and, *You're Never Too Old To Dream Dare Dance!*

www.janfraserbusinesstraining.com
www.janfraser.com

SECTION 4: CHAPTER 1

Unsinkability

by Jan Fraser

> *"The best part of life is not just surviving, but thriving with passion and compassion and humor and style and generosity and kindness."* Maya Angelou

Simply Hang on!

My father shocked my mother when I was nine years old. He went to work one day and came home with a boat he had bought secondhand from a co-worker. It was a 16-foot, wooden boat with a 40-horsepower motor. She was a classic beauty!

"You bought a boat and didn't discuss it with me first?" asked Mom. My parents always conferred on large purchases because we were a middle-class family with three daughters and no money for extras.

"This boat is going to keep our family together," reasoned Dad. He thought with a boat, we would take our friends on outings and it would keep us from getting into 'teen trouble.'

"All of you (I had two older sisters) will learn how to water ski!" he announced. That was a big statement coming from a man who never learned to swim.

For our first lake outing our parents invited their dear friends, Mr. and Mrs. Hughes, to join us. The Hughes owned a boat and were experienced skiers. They promised our parents they would get all of us up on skis at Indian Lake, Ohio, a reservoir near our home.

I was small and so were my feet. I needed to wear tennis shoes inside the rubber ski shoes to fit. As I lowered my skinny little body into the chilly lake waters with my life vest buckled tightly around my neck, I felt like a daredevil ready to conquer the high-wire at the circus. I was not a swimmer in those days, more of a dog-paddler. Encouraged by my family and the Hughes, I really thought I could ski that first time out.

"Hang on. Just hang on," Mrs. Hughes shouted over the engine idling noise. I shivered and looked searchingly into her eyes from the shifting waters behind the boat.

"You'll be fine," she encouraged. Hearing Mrs. Hughes's words echoing in my head, I was determined to do it. It was simple. All I had to do was "hang on." Dad started the engine slowly, at first. I felt the eventual tug of my towrope pulling me through the water and I was beginning to stand up. I remember saying to myself, "I can do this."

Then, the engine revved and I was wobbly in an effort to stand up. To my amazement I was skiing or at least I thought I was. I was still holding onto the towrope so that was good, right? Not the case at all. I was face down in the water holding on like Mrs. Hughes told me to do. Unfortunately, the skis had blown out from under me and I was skiing flat across the lake with my face submerged in the water still wearing my tennis shoes. I pulled my head up to take a breath and realized I was skiing lying down not vertically as most people do. Eventually, I let go of the towrope and Dad brought the boat around to pick me up. Mrs. Hughes, with help from my family, hauled me back into the boat and we had a good laugh about it.

After that day, I decided I was really going to do it. And I did get up on skis the next time we went to the lake. Over the years, I learned to ski on two skis, on one ski, cross the wake, and to ski tandem with my sister. Dad was right. That boat did keep our family together with countless happy memories. It was my first recorded experience of being 'unsinkable.'

Smiling now as I recall that first ski outing when I resembled a human torpedo, I realize that hanging on was as important then as it is now. Hanging on is what we do when we must overcome, survive, get up, over, and through whatever is challenging us in our lives. It is a characteristic of being unsinkable and builds self-esteem and character. If you can hang on through it, you grow from it.

The following situations called for unsinkability in my life:

· When I needed a job to have the money to support my daughters, no matter how difficult the boss...
· When I received a scary medical diagnosis...
· When my daughter was run over by a motorbike in front of my eyes...
· When I jumped out of a plane at 14,000 feet...
· When panic was my first response and I couldn't allow myself to go there...

What situations have called for unsinkability in your life? People find that when they hang in and manage their emotions and themselves through difficult situations, their self-esteem blossoms. Each time you found courage to face what you didn't think you could, you built unsinkable genes by taking action. These genes grew and developed inside you and helped you step up the next time it became critical to do so.

I know you have unsinkability genes. You discover them each time you stretch further than you thought you could. Those stretching opportunities result in key memories that you can recall when faced with a new challenge.

I say to myself, "If I did that, then I can do this." Relive the strengths that you called upon to hang on. Celebrate them and you. Remember you will not sink if you simply hang on!

> *"No matter how you define success, you will need to be resilient, empowered, authentic, and limber to get there."* Joanie Connell

Unsinkable Mentor Mom

Sadie Beverly Woroshilsky became a nurse even though her father forbade it. She disobeyed him in 1931 and commenced nurse's training. With no money for schooling, she enrolled in a work-study program at the hospital and graduated with her Registered Nursing Degree. Her father, from Russia, believed daughters needed to get married and have children. But she knew nursing was her life purpose and nothing could have shaken her from that path. Years later, he did come to value her degree: when he broke his leg and needed a private nurse. Sadie flew thousands of miles across the country to take care of him. It was then that he realized how wrong he had been.

Sadie was my mother. She was a star in my universe. Her legacy of selflessness and unsinkability continues to this day in my sisters, my daughters, my grandchildren, and me.

Later in life, Mom had health issues. She fractured both hips at the same time, fell and shattered her elbow, which prevented her from lifting her arm high enough to comb her hair, and survived breast cancer with radical mastectomies. Through it all, she was a survivor.

During difficult times I lean on her unsinkability when I ask myself, "What advice would Mom give me in this situation?" What course of action would she recommend? Even though Mom has been gone over 24 years, I continue to call upon her spirit in times of challenge.

> *"Tell me and I forget, teach me and I may remember, involve me and I learn."* Margaret Mead

Do you have a star, mentor, or coach for unsinkability in your life? Is there someone you can rely on for strength in times of trial? If you don't, start searching for your mentor today. We can model a characteristic, an action plan, and a path to create greater success in our lives based on inspiration from mentors, guides, coaches, and counselors whether they are family, friends, or even famous people.

Unsinkable We

> *"What I learned was the quality of continual reinvention."* Merrie Spaeth

I grew up petrified to speak.

There was no need for me to talk because my older sisters spoke for me. Eventually, they graduated from high school and I was on my own to speak for myself.

I gathered courage and continued my education, overcoming shyness to receive diplomas from high school and college.

I married while still in college and missed my graduation ceremony because my first daughter was born that same week. Graduating from the University of Cincinnati with a Bachelor's Degree in Sociology was a major accomplishment and helped me understand the behavior of people in groups.

I felt unsinkable...that is, until I allowed divorce to pull me down into a sea of guilt and worthlessness. I was on my own, scared, far from family, and the sole supporter of my two little girls.

Because I had braces on my teeth and wore a full head gear cap 24 hours a day, I believed the nearby orthodontist was the only employer who would hire me: I was not a pretty sight. Applying for that first grown-up job after graduating college and being a full-time mom was terrifying. My friend gave me a bright red suit, that I wore to the interview. She told me she got the job every time she wore it and I was hoping that suit would get the job for me, too.

My daughters were counting on me as we received only $200 per month child support. They had faith in me that I didn't have in myself. I called the orthodontic office each week to see if they had made a decision. The last time I called, the receptionist told me sadly that I wasn't selected. I remember getting off the phone not wanting my daughters to see my tears of defeat.

Then, seconds later, the phone rang again. It was the same receptionist telling me how sorry she was. She had made a mistake. I was the one who had gotten the job! Hallelujah! My daughters and I danced around our living room with delight. I dried my tears and celebrated.

I was sure it was my daughters' unsinkable faith and the get-the-job red suit that secured the position for me.

Does something you wear help you feel unsinkable on the outside when you are shaking on the inside? Every woman needs an unsinkable suit of armor to wear on occasions when extreme courage is needed or until her own unsinkability kicks in.

Our feeling of unsinkability can ebb and flow like the ocean. Sometimes you plan to be unsinkable and then get knocked down with waves coming ashore. There may be someone to help you get back up, like my daughters in this instance, or a supportive friend. You can borrow from others until you get your unsinkability back and continue building it again.

Keep your goals in front of you, put your red suit on, and don't take 'no' for an answer. You will find your voice. That was my experience when I answered an ad in the Los Angeles Times that read, "Work part time, Fly free."

Again wearing my red suit, I got the job at Eastern and later, Delta Air Lines. I fulfilled my passion by engaging in exceptional customer service and supporting others. I even had a red airline jacket. All was going well in my airline career until my mother's condition worsened and I needed to transfer to San Diego to be near her.

Unfortunately, the only position in San Diego with Delta was on the airport ramp loading bags into the belly of the aircraft. It was the hardest manual labor I have ever done in my life. I felt like crawling out of work every day on my hands and knees because my legs were wilted carrot sticks.

One day, working along side a male co-worker in the hot belly of a 727 aircraft, I felt like I was coming apart. It was my bra strap breaking from the physical exertion of stacking the heavy bags neatly in rows.

I wished I had been working with a woman. At least I could have told her and we both would have had a good laugh. I was unprepared for the intense discrimination I endured from a male co-worker while working on that ramp.

He hated all women and since I was a woman, he hated me. He delighted in seeing me struggle with heavy boxes of fish packed in ice. He hoped I would hurt my back and be out of his sight on medical leave for a while. I persevered. I would not allow one man to break me or damage my unsinkability genes.

Have you faced discrimination on the job or in life? Worked with someone who wanted you to fail? If you haven't, you probably know someone who has. It can be paralyzing and make your life miserable. What options do you have?

I worried and stewed about it and finally decided to face him and speak up. In that conversation, I helped him see that if I sustained an injury I would be on the ramp forever with him. He said, "I see what you mean."

After that, he left me alone and weeks later, I was moved upstairs to the ticket counter where I was better suited to the work. We both won, which was my purpose in speaking to him. It also gave me validation that I hadn't lost the unsinkability gene and it was showing up again after divorce and discrimination.

Throughout your life, focus on keeping your unsinkable genes activated.

If you don't feel that you have them yet, there are several ways to get the unsinkable gene into your DNA even if you didn't inherit it from a family member or friend ...

1. Absorb it from coaches, mentors, training and/or environments;

2. Develop it from passion, spirituality, experiences and/or adventures;

3. Emulate it from reading books, listening to powerful messages, and attending success seminars.

We need to speak up for ourselves and 'hang in there' until we can create a better situation. For me, that event was becoming a flight attendant at age 43. It was a dream job and it didn't happen overnight. I did everything I could to get that job, including enrolling in a Spanish immersion class at the junior college, visiting a dentist to improve my smile, changing my hairstyle, and observing how professional flight attendants performed.

When you want success badly enough, research to determine what you need to do to make it happen, and then do it. I wore an emerald green suit and got the job anyway. My feeling of unsinkability soared and now I was making my own magic. Years later, I took an early retirement from American Airlines to pursue speaking full time and writing books.

The affirmation, "I am speaking with confidence and clarity to everyone I meet," has propelled me forward in times of hesitation or fear with public speaking. Another example of a daily success affirmation I have used is, "I am unsinkable today and achieving all that I choose for my life's success." If you don't have a positive personal statement that helps you feel unsinkable, work to create one.

> *Forget, "I can't do that!"*
> *Replace it with, "I will do that!"*

Looking back, every step I have taken to arrive at this place in time has encompassed the aspects of 'unsinkability.' It has taken me from painfully shy girl to world-class speaker, author, trainer, and coach and has created countless opportunities to move forward in my personal life and career.

I recognize and celebrate unsinkability in women all over the world who share their stories, dreams, and goals with me.

We can do anything we choose to do if we are driven by passion for our work, cultivate our unsinkable gene, and ask for mentoring, as needed, along the way. I am living proof.

Remember...

You are unsinkable; together we are unstoppable.

Wherever you are, feel supported by this community of caring, victorious women who want you to succeed in living your highest life purpose.

The World is Ours. Let's Go for It!
Unsinkable We!

Success Strategies

1. *Believe in yourself* and your instinctive ability to hang on!

2. *Use the lessons gained* from each life experience to move forward with strength. Remember, "If I did THAT, I can do THIS!"

3. *Seek a mentor* that is an example of unsinkability and encourages you to live the life you choose to create. "What would Mom do or say in this situation?"

4. *Borrow your courage.* Put on your 'red suit' and lean on someone stronger until you can walk on your own.

5. *Keep yourself focused with affirmations.* Repeat them daily as a constant reminder of your life goals and a way to implant them in your mind.

6. *Become a life-long student.* Realize the benefit of learning from others by reading, attending training, or seeking a coach.

Carol Talbot

Carol Talbot has guided and inspired people in more than 18 countries, offering motivating events for world class companies globally.

A professional speaker, Carol is a Master Trainer and respected authority on NLP and Founder of The Y.O.U. Code. Based in Dubai, she's often called 'the FIRE-STARTER' as she 'fires up' individuals and teams teaching them how to walk across burning hot coals of around 1,700 degrees Fahrenheit.

Author of **Breaking Through,** Carol has a passion for empowering others to go out into the world and "be the difference that makes the difference!"

www.caroltalbot.me
www.matrix-training.com
www.nlpuncovered.com

SECTION 4: CHAPTER 2

Life-long Learning

by Carol Talbot

"Learning is a treasure that will follow its owner everywhere." Chinese Proverb

I held my breath as the bright orange burning hot coals glistened in the dark just a few inches from my bare feet. All through the day I kept hoping they would get to the part where they would say "it's cool as moss" or put us in a trance and have us chant "it's cool as ice." But they didn't. They just kept telling us how hot the coals would be.

We had built the fire a few hours earlier and as the sun went down, so did the fire, and now we were left with burning hot coals of about 1,700 degrees Fahrenheit ready for our first fire-walking experience. One by one, I watched other fire-walkers make their way across those burning hot coals until there I was...looking down at the hot coals. That's the moment I heard a loud voice inside my head saying, "Are you nuts, Carol?" I had an image of my feet black and charred...and it was as if my whole life flashed before me.

When I was at school I envied friends who had already decided on a career and life path. I never knew who I wanted to be or what I wanted to do. That meant exploring a lot of different career paths...selling advertising for magazines, recruitment consulting, promotion work, and even spraying people with perfume in department stores. I'd get bored with most jobs in less than a year and move on. I remember a conversation with one manager as I handed in another resignation letter. She said, "Carol, you're never going to get anywhere if you keep changing jobs." However, what I did have was curiosity and a thirst for learning.

Fast forward the years and quite a few more different jobs. This time it was a country shift. I'm often asked what brought me to Dubai in the Middle East. In truth, I was in a ten year relationship with a man who I thought was the love of my life. As it turned out, I wasn't the love of *his* life. I was devastated when the relationship came to a close. It felt like a part of me had come to a close...a close in a chapter of my life. Months later, I was still devastated and going through the motions of work, home, eat, and sleep.

Among other things, a meditation group became a saving grace. When you meditate or use a hypnotic trance induction, you partially suspend the conscious minds' analyzing, criticizing, judging, and beating yourself up, which allows you to connect and communicate with your subconscious mind. In meditation you literally slow your brain waves down, which allows you to be privy to information that only happens when you are in that brain wave cycle. In fact, most mystical experiences happen when your brain waves are in theta, which for most of us is a feeling of drowsiness.

It was during meditation that I realized it was time to make a decision. A *decision is an opportunity to exercise your options and choices.* I decided that I had been gifted an opportunity for re-invention and so I started to seek opportunities overseas.

Fuelled by the desire to move forward, I contacted everyone I knew overseas. There were auditions and job applications sent here, there, and everywhere. For weeks, a flurry of activity! Yet nothing happened. Having exhausted all avenues and feeling frustrated, my mother wisely told me that if I was absolutely sure that I'd done everything possible, that I had left no stone unturned, and taken as much action as possible, then all that needed to be done was to simply allow the universe to respond. And respond it did!

Looking back, that one decision created a number of challenges, a lot of incredible opportunities, and some truly amazing experiences. Another journey of discovery and learning had begun. This is what drives me to continually seek opportunities to be a life-long learner and encourage gorgeous women like you to make that shift, too.

Are you growing or dying?

Everything on this planet is either growing or dying so choosing to be on the 'growing' side of that equation, I'm a self-confessed course junkie. I've read thousands of books and attended a lot of personal development courses, too— all the 'ologies and 'erapies—in my quest and passion for knowledge, understanding, guidance, wisdom, learning, and development. This quest and thirst within has led me to meet amazing mentors, role models, teachers, and friends, so it felt natural to move into the field of training, learning, and development. And so it was, that half-way through delivering a training program to thirty-plus delegates from leading organizations in the region, the session came to an abrupt halt as I found myself being arrested by the labor department and taken to the local police station. Can you imagine that!

In challenging situations, I have learned to ask myself, "is this a *crisis* or an *opportunity?*" Well, every cloud has a silver lining, as that situation proved to be the catalyst to setting up my own business. In addition, one of the delegates on that program was so impressed with how I handled the situation, she recommended me to her organization and they became my first client, offering me a retainer contract for three years.

Now I run my own successful business and own two properties mortgage-free; I've spoken in over 17 countries including a TEDx™ talk to over 1,000 people; I'm author of an Amazon best-seller, and as an NLP Master Trainer I've helped thousands of people through our transformational programs and incredible breakthrough events like the fire-walk.

'Going' through the process or 'growing' through the process?

Each year I take time to consider how I can best encourage and fulfill my own learning and development. However, at the end of 2011, I found myself to be 'mind-full' rather than 'mindful.' After going through more training programs it felt like I was *going* through the process rather than *growing* through the process.

> *It's not always about acquiring more knowledge, learning more, or achieving more: it's often in the letting go that we can allow ourselves to BE with the flow!*

The following year became known as 'my year of unlearning.' Discarding notebooks and note-taking for hiking boots and a good camera, I headed into the heart and lungs of the world for what has become one of the defining trips of my life...and I've travelled a lot!

Deep in the Ecuador rainforest lives one of the few indigenous tribes to ever reach out to the West. Not because they need us; quite the reverse. The Achuar tribe has reached out in an unprecedented effort to preserve their land, their way of life and, more importantly, to educate us on the real damage our consumer and 'got to have more' lifestyle has done.

There is a huge misconception that indigenous people are uneducated and poor in many ways. I discovered that nothing could be farther from the truth. These people are not primitive nor savage. In fact, they have a wisdom and joy for life that far exceeds our world of technology.

As well as an opportunity to connect with 'Pachamama' (Mother Earth) and communicate with nature—especially when there is a tree growing in the middle of your room—there is much beauty and opportunity for learning while being part of a group travelling together. At times, you will be uncomfortable, angry, irritated at others, yet there is much to learn when you allow yourself to notice what comes up.

Givers Gain

You could suspect that a group of professional speakers travelling together in Asia would be a recipe for clashing egos and competition for the spotlight.

Together We Can Change the World has a mission to provide educational opportunities to orphans and make a profound difference in a child's life in South East Asia. As well as 'speaking for our keep,' we also had the opportunity to put a leadership and service excellence summit together to raise funds in Cambodia. It was a beautiful experience as we all pulled together for a larger cause—checking lighting, sound systems, seating arrangements, and the stage set as well as re-booting crashing laptops for one of our colleagues who was on stage at the time!

Our intention was to help, contribute and serve others. In organizations, this would be termed Corporate Social Responsibility (CSR)—when you give you gain so much more. Whether that be in opening your heart, developing leadership skills, or having the ability to be part of a team, the rewards are phenomenal when you practice *PSR: Personal Social Responsibility.*

'Givers Gain' is the philosophy behind Business Networking International (BNI), a phenomenally successful organization that offers powerful opportunities to share ideas, learn, and grow through networking successfully. You've probably heard that saying, "it's not what you know, it's who you know." As a past educational coordinator for one of the millions of chapters around the globe. I've learned that it's a great way to sharpen your ability to build trust and credibility of you, your products, and your services in less than 60 seconds in a memorable way once a week.

Although I'm no longer affiliated with a chapter, two years later I still collaborate with the many successful entrepreneurs I connected with at that time.

Your level of success is dependent on your level of thinking and the people you choose to surround yourself with. Are you inspired by the people around you right now?

Learning comes in many shapes, forms, and disguises!

As a very healthy woman, waking up one morning in excruciating pain was a complete shock, both mentally and physically.

Desiccated discs in my neck pressed against nerves that shot pain down my left arm and left my fingers numb! Yoga did not help and exacerbated the problem. Visits to a chiropractor, an acupuncturist, and a specialist yielded zero results, failing to alleviate the pain and lessen my tears.

There is always a point and purpose to pain, and my belief is that it is a strong signal from deep within the body's intelligence that our emotional health is out of balance. Huge lessons flowed in the form of asking and receiving, vulnerability (and how powerful that is), and allowing myself to be open and receive.

Caught in the quiet of meditation I found the opportunity to draw inwards, to listen and learn, reflect and know that when the purpose of the suffering is complete, healing takes place and we are energized again.

We learn through looking within and when we can recognize ourselves as our own creation, we then free ourselves from the fear of living a less than satisfying life and expand the horizons of our beliefs and stretch our heart, mind, and the *boundaries of what is possible.*

Be more than you thought you could be!

As a master fire-walk instructor, I wanted to learn from the best. Peggy Dylan is affectionately known as the 'mother of the western fire-walking movement.' Travelling by plane, train, car, and bus, I finally reached the retreat center on the French-Swiss border for certification training. One glance at the very bold and 'in your face' waiver form—and, to be honest—if I could have found a bus, a car, plane, or train I would have been on it and swiftly departed!

In addition to fire-walking, we also had an opportunity to participate in a sweat lodge ceremony. I was horrified when the group elected for a naked sweat lodge. For goodness sake, being British, it's just not the 'done thing.' Taking an act of courage, I was the only one wearing a bikini and a sarong! The fire-walking ceremonies also entailed an act of courage (although we were not naked).

So I paused to allow myself to BE in the flow for a moment. I changed the voice inside my head, and summoned an image of what I would look like if I were totally successful. Taking a deep breath in...and out, I walked purposefully across those burning hot coals of 1,700 degrees Fahrenheit like a person who knows exactly where they are going.

As I reached the cool grass the other side of the hot coals I looked down and could see that my feet were black. Rushing to a nearby tap I washed and examined them thoroughly. There was not a mark on them! Anyone looking at me at that moment would have said "Wow, now there's a person who can do just about anything!"

Today, I regularly run fire-walks and I'm often asked why I run these powerful breakthrough events—after all, does the world need more fire-walkers? To be honest, the answer is "probably not." However, what the world does need, and what YOU need to be truly successful, is to face your fears and to let go of everything that is holding you back.

The fire-walk inspires that sort of courage in people... it certainly inspired courage in me and continues to act as a reminder of just how powerful we really are. It's the quickest way to shift your "can't do's" to "can do's," tap into your potential, and *be more than you thought you could be!*

It's impossible not to learn!

What I have learned is that it is impossible not to learn!

One of the reasons I created the 'Y.O.U. Code Experience' is simply to create an opportunity to ignite and engage each other in the evolution of a different perspective. It is an ever expanding conversation in a direction that many have not previously gone. It allows us to step into a fuller focus of who we are.

On the road of life—whether it is through journaling your experiences...be they good, bad, or ugly—hiring a coach or mentor, travelling, attending training programs, networking, meditating, reading, watching movies or a documentary, spending time with friends, family or strangers, or out in nature, there is always more to learn and discover!

Our true purpose, and to feel purpose-full, is to simply evolve and expand our wakefulness, awareness, and consciousness!

Success Strategies

① Decisions are *opportunities* to exercise your options and choices. What decisions do you need to make right now?

② Are you growing through your experiences? Are you getting the results you want? Is it time to *change* to get better results based on past experience?

③ Are you going through the process or *growing* through the process? What do you need to let go of? What is no longer serving you?

④ *Givers Gain.* How are you making a contribution in the world and to those around you?

⑤ Be MORE than you think you can be. Move your "can't do's" to "CAN do's!"

Amina Makhdoom

Amina's background in corporate America combined with her extensive training in human potential allows her to deliver cutting-edge information in a manner that resonates clearly with business audiences.

Her mission is to leave you with a clear objective, tangible actions to reach the next step, and inspiration and personal realization of your own power. She focuses on helping you reveal within yourself your ability to achieve extraordinary results.

Amina is affectionately labeled 'A Ray of Sunshine' not only for her positive attitude and disposition, but for her warmth and ability to connect with each person in the room, creating a space that allows for growth.

www.fresnelconsult.com

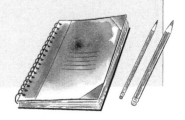

SECTION 4: CHAPTER 3

0% Effort, 100% Return.

by Amina Makhdoom

> *"Nature's intelligence functions with effortless ease...with carefreeness, harmony, and love. And when we harness the forces of harmony, joy, and love, we create success and good fortune with effortless ease."*
> *Deepak Chopra*

What if I told you that you could get everything you wanted in life with no effort? In fact, what if I told you the secret to realizing your biggest dreams is to follow your joy and live life in a 'State of Ease?' Does this sound too good to be true? Well, it is possible and here is why: effort is a pushing energy; it includes exertion and is focused on achievement. We live in a society where all of these qualities are rewarded. True accomplishment occurs only when we stop pushing and start living joyfully.

Getting off the Hamster Wheel

My father wanted me to be financially independent and free so he taught me good values that would get me there: hard work, effort, pushing myself to learn more and do more. Becoming the perfect, Type A child helped me achieve many accolades and garnered me a lot of positive attention. However, it didn't bring me as much joy as I thought it would bring.

This continued into college. When I started my career with a prestigious consulting company I was very impressive. With each achievement, I felt like I had to work harder to maintain it. I was on the hamster wheel with no end in sight.

Seven years into my career as a Management Consultant, I was beyond burned out. I remember my father, a Federal Government employee and immigrant, telling me that companies do not expect you to work more than 40 hours. He said, "they will think you are slow and cannot get your work done in 40 hours." It was funny at the time, because he didn't understand I was part of a machine that took kids out of college and worked them hard for two years. At that two-year mark, half the young consultants quit and the other half worked even harder. I was one of those that worked harder.

It was a badge of honor to respond to requests in the middle of the night or to work a 70-hour week. I was considered a top performer—a 'Go-To' girl. Everyone knew they could count on me—I was dedicated and rewarded in my career. I was exhausted and not happy, but…I was making good money and considered a top performer by my peers and my managers. I assumed this was a good thing and that I was going places.

One day, I fell off the path of perfection. I went through a bad break-up that left me sad all the time. All of a sudden, the career and all the perks lost their shine. The perfect life I had planned had huge cracks in it, and I had no idea how to repair them. I was smart enough to know this would pass. However, I was barely able to keep up appearances and perform my job.

In a moment of deep dissatisfaction, I wrote down all the things that I wanted in my ideal life (the life that I was nowhere near living). I wrote that I did not want to work a traditional 'nine to five' job nor be stuck at a desk. I wanted to take a yoga class in the middle of the day; I wanted to work from home; I wanted to help improve the community; I wanted to work with children and parents; and the list continued. Oh, and I wanted to do all of this while working half as many hours and making double the amount of money I was currently making.

Within two years, I was doing all of that. I was working half the hours and making double my salary. Everyone asks me how I did it—but I really did not know. Realizing that I had achieved something amazing yet never feeling like I had worked to achieve it, I, too, wanted to know how this happened. When I realized I was living my dream life, it seemed like it just happened, almost like it was magical. But, it was not magical. There were some specific joyful, happy, self-care steps I took to get me off the hamster wheel and onto a path of loving my life.

I have come to realize that no one achieves their big goals in a negative state. That means no one gets their dream while they are exhausted, burned out, miserable, angry, or tired. If you feel this way, you are actually farther away from your dream than you think, even if you are doing ten action steps a day to achieve it. That is what I did not know—it was not about what I *did* but *how I was feeling* (how I was *being*) that helped me achieve the huge successes in life.

I could muscle my way through anything, just like most people, but the consistent, happy achievement that flows into life came when I *stopped* muscling and *started* being joyful. Given my background in process consulting and corporate training, I reviewed what I had done and realized there were three key ingredients that I changed in my life which helped me obtain this amazing success. These few actions, practiced regularly, had a *huge* impact on my ability to create my dream life.

My First Key

The first ingredient was listing all the elements I wanted in my life—these are the ones that brought me joy!

I did not know it at the time, but listing all the things I wanted in my life was like creating a vision board, except I created mine with words instead of images. I let my imagination run free and thought if I could live my ideal dream life, what would I do? These were not necessarily work activities but activities I enjoyed such as dance class, yoga, going for walks, and spending time with my nieces and nephews.

During my burnout period, I spent a lot of time with family members since that was nurturing for me. I had three nieces and nephews at the time, and I went to soccer games, school events, and volunteered to read in their classrooms. All these activities made me happy and brought me great joy! They never felt like another item on my To-Do list, but projects that I got excited about and could not wait to do.

One of the secrets I learned is that the most successful leaders do not exert force; instead, they focus clearly on what they want—believing fully that they will achieve it—and they follow their joy. This is part of the beautiful gift of feminine energy: being clear in what we want and allowing it to come to us without exerting force. When we ignore this feminine energy by pushing and achieving instead of allowing, it can have detrimental effects on us, especially on our health and mental well-being.

Today I see more female executives who are not following their joy. Their reason: they simply do not have the time. The less they follow their joy, the harder it is for them to achieve their goal.

The fastest way to achieve a goal does not involve effort, but rather, belief that the goal *can be* and *will be* achieved while taking care of yourself and finding paths that bring you joy.

My Second Key

The second ingredient was to focus on feelings rather than actions.

As an overachiever, this was a shocker for me! What I was doing was much less important than how I was feeling! The actions are unimportant. Read that again: *the actions are unimportant.* What *is* important is the *feeling,* the *belief,* the *being.* The *doing* is negligible in comparison.

After I listed all of the things I wanted in my life, I hung a massive list of them on my wall. I never really looked at it again, though I probably subconsciously saw it every day because it was hanging in a central place in my apartment. Two years later, when I was cleaning my room, I went to take it down.

As I was removing it from the wall two years later, I realized I had achieved every single item I had written on the poster. The actions were unimportant to me. However, the time I spent writing down what I wanted, the feeling of freedom and joy in creating that list was meaningful. I vividly imagined that life and miraculously transformed my situation into achieving my dream existence.

I went to a lot of social events because I felt like I was 'supposed to' or I 'should.' I have always had a lot of friends, and I never wanted anyone to feel like they were not important to me. This sometimes meant going to lunch with one group of friends, followed by a baby shower, followed by dinner with another group of friends. My weekends were booked usually to the minute. Even though all these activities were 'fun,' I was not having fun because I was so stressed trying to get them all in.

That bad break-up was my excuse to sit in bed for hours on end and watch countless re-runs of The Gilmore Girls on televsion.

I went for hour-long walks every day, sometimes multiple times a day. I said 'no' to almost every invitation that came my way (which was crazy for me) and spent long periods of time with myself, my family, or really close friends. I realized, I was having fun! Despite the pain and the sadness, I was happier because I was following my joy.

I am back to a busy social calendar again, but now I only say 'yes' to the events that sound like fun, instead of seeing how many people I can please in one weekend. This one item of being more focused on how I felt than what I did had a *huge* impact on the successes in my life.

My Third Key

The third key ingredient was taking great care of myself, and each of us knows exactly what this means for us.

For me, I decided to say 'no' to social invitations; but you may decide to say 'yes' to social invitations. This will look completely different for each of us, but the key is knowing how to be kinder, gentler, and more loving to ourselves and only we can do that.

In my heartbroken state, I only had energy for activities that soothed me temporarily. I was an overachiever who was leaving work early to go for walks; I was sure I was having a nervous breakdown. I did not learn this in the positive context of achieving my dreams through ease; I learned it through sheer mental and emotional exhaustion.

During this time, I started treating myself to high-quality ice cream, fresh smoothies, long baths, trips to see girlfriends from college, and even a trip to Barbados. I felt nurtured. My parents lived close by, and I had a lot of evening teas with my mom. In general, I moved slower. I cleared my calendar, and only added activities that felt nurturing and caring. For the first time in my life, I took care of myself the way I take care of all the other people in my life. I treated myself the way I treat my best friends and family. I gave myself permission to buy the lavender-scented bath crystals, sit and cry, or to go for my second walk of the day.

I learned how to be my own best friend.

Testing My Three Keys

Once I came up with these three keys, I decided to test them to ensure they worked (without a heartache attached). I took a year to see if—by following my joy, not worrying about specific actions or exerting effort, and taking great care of myself—I could make the same amount of money as the previous year.

Since this was a test, I went all out. I slowed down and asked myself each day, "what do you want to do? What will bring you the greatest joy?" And, I did it.

And...to my surprise, I made *more* money than the previous year, while working fewer overall hours, and spending more time doing things that brought me joy!

Since that time (five years ago), I have consistently made more each year while working significantly fewer hours than the year before. I only say 'yes' to work I really want to do, so it does not feel like work. I do a lot of work for free because I love what I do and, somehow, the money keeps showing up. But, I know now, if I chased the money or tried to force something to happen, it would not work nearly as well as doing what I love and trusting that it will all work out financially.

In yoga, there is a philosophy about balancing between ease and effort. I have found this philosophy to apply not only to yoga, but to all areas of life. There is a time for action—and, when that time comes, it feels good to take the action; it does not feel like effort.

Do you have moments where you are working harder than ever before (which appears to the outside world as putting in tons of effort), but it doesn't feel like you are working at all? Think of a time when you felt that way: were you feeling stressed and exhausted or joyful and exhilarated? *That is what 0% effort, 100% return means.* It does not mean you will never work hard again. It just means that when you are working hard, it will not feel like it. There is no strain, exertion, exhaustion—it will be joyful.

On a Mission

Given my results, I am on a mission to help every woman achieve her dreams while taking excellent care of herself!

Take a moment and ask yourself, "In my life, is it possible for me to do less and get more done? Is it possible for me to let go and allow it to miraculously get done? Is it possible for me to do what makes me happy and be totally successful?" What answer did you get? I have proven in my life, time and time again, that the answer to all of these questions is a loud, resounding "YES!"

While these three ingredients sound easy enough, it takes discipline to apply them in a way to get astounding results. We have been trained to *go, go, go,* and it takes applied mindfulness to practice relaxing and enjoying. To support you in your practice, review the **Success University for Women**™ - **Wisdom Working for You Companion Workbook, Volume 1** and complete a 30-day challenge to apply these three ingredients to achieve your goals while following your joy.

On a deeper level, when you create in a state of joy, you create from your heart. The universe responds and opens up to you making your path easier. The world needs your love, joy and clear intentions. We can't get there if we are too exhausted to share our joy and light with the world.

So, go easy on yourself. Do less, rest more, take walks, smile, laugh, be happy, and know that you are *accomplishing* more by doing those things than you could possibly imagine.

Then, allow the magical force of the world to easily, effortlessly bring your biggest dreams to you!

Success Strategies

Success University for Women™

1. Realize true *accomplishment* occurs when you are in a state of joy.

2. When faced with a choice, always choose the one that will bring you the *most joy.*

3. Trust that, *when you are happy,* the Universe will meet you 90% of the way to achieve your goals.

4. Believe in the *power of ease over effort.*

5. Know that taking *great care of yourself* will get you farther in life than anything else.

Notes

Jacqueline Throop-Robinson

Jacqueline is an author, speaker, and CEO of Spark Engagement. Over the last 25 years, Jacqueline has worked with thousands of leaders and employees in more than 20 countries supporting passion, productivity, and performance.

She is the author of an Amazon best-seller, *Fire Up Your Team, 50 Ways for Leaders to Connect, Collaborate and Create with their Teams* (2013).

As a feminist, Jacqueline mentors and supports women in life and work. Jacqueline holds a BA, BFA, and MA as well as numerous certifications.

Jacqueline lives in Halifax, Canada, with her spouse, Evan, and two children, Taylor and Jamie.

www.spark-engagement.com

SECTION 4: CHAPTER 4

Purpose, Progress and Passions

by Jacqueline Throop-Robinson

> *"I think we have been conditioned to think of passion as a scarce and elusive luxury: when, in fact, we each have the capacity to be passionate about something. I think our passions await us, like a faithful friend, ever present, even when ignored."* Ivy Kusinga, Philadelphia

When I was 12, I was the tallest girl in my class. I looked grown up and wanted to be grown up. That summer of 1977, I decided I wanted to to get a job. The year before, my Mom had paid me $5.00 per week to clean our house while she herself did housework for elderly people. But I wanted to test the waters in the 'real world.' My father, who was a caretaker at an historic property called Marshlands Inn, spoke to the owners, and they offered me a job washing dishes.

Most people wouldn't be excited about washing dishes, but I couldn't wait to start! Then the reality set in.

For the entire summer I stood at a hot dishwasher, emptying a never-ending parade of trays of fine china, hand-washing and drying mounds of sterling silver, and scrubbing the encrusted Baked Scallops and Lobster Newburg baking dishes—all for minimum wage, a whopping $2.85 per hour! My feet hurt, I was hot and sweaty most of the time, and my eczema went crazy so that even rubber gloves didn't help. Nevertheless, if you'd asked me, "How do you like working at Marshlands?" without missing a beat I would have said, "I love it!" Best of all, I would have meant it.

At 12 years old, in less than ideal conditions, I experienced passion at work. However, it wasn't until many years later that I truly understood that the choices I made then and the choices I would make later were the reason I could always find passion in all facets of my life.

(1) Focus on What's Meaningful: Start from Within

Pay attention to your natural interests.

Growing up in a small university town of 3,500 people who were often divided along religious and ethnic lines (Catholic vs. Protestant and English vs. French), there was no shortage of people willing to tell you what to think, believe, and do; what to study, where to work, and how to amuse. It was easy to be guided by others' choices rather than your own, and it wasn't until I attended university that I began listening to my inner guide.

On the first day of classes, all students were required to register for their programs. As I approached the head of the line, I faced a deepening dilemma: I had always done well in school and the conventional wisdom of the time dictated I pursue studies in Science. Left to my own devices, however, I loved to draw, sing, and read. I began to imagine myself in Science lectures and labs instead of reading and writing. I took a deep breath and said 'no' to Physics and 'yes' to English.

I was terrified and exhilarated at the same time, but I knew where my natural interests lay. I had chosen in favor of those interests and by doing so I was activating intrinsic motivators. I would not need to force myself to attend class or do the work required; it would not be a slog to get through school. I wanted to read the novels; I wanted to understand literary criticism; and I wanted to learn more about the human condition.

During the term there were certainly days I didn't feel like getting up for my 8:30 a.m. classes, but by choosing topics that excited me, it was not the uphill battle I witnessed in others. Did I worry about the future? No. I simply enjoyed the university experience and the process of learning.

Move from interests and curiosity to aspiration.

I knew I wanted to make a difference—I wasn't sure what this would look like, but the desire to make a positive impact and a contribution were driving forces within me. I was aware of a connection to a higher purpose. It is natural for humans to progress from childhood play and discovery to an awareness of one's aspirations.

Coming out of graduate school, I stumbled into a corporate training job for the postal service. The money and travel were appealing and "How hard could it be to teach people how to lick a stamp?" I joked with my roommates.

Little did I know I would have to familiarize myself with cutting-edge technology and over one-hundred products and services—some of them quite complex. I would also have to teach seasoned, sometimes resistant, employees. I was immediately humbled, but I thrived on the challenge! Through this experience, I discovered true ambition.

One day at a small postal outlet in Winnipeg, I noticed one of the retail employees, June, a woman of 55 years of age, becoming increasingly anxious as a queue formed in the store and her technologically inexperienced fingers began to fumble. As I approached her, I saw tears well up in her eyes. "June, take your time. You know this," I said. I took over the support tasks and let her concentrate on the system. I continued to coach her through the process. We moved the queue and when we were able to take a break, June exclaimed, "I did it!"

From that moment on, I knew I loved supporting others in their learning. The day had been exhausting, but I left the store feeling completely energized. I had discovered a goal that I would serve for decades to come. I also came to realize that this work was just like my dishwashing job! Truly. It contained all the same drivers of passion that I had first experienced as a 12 year old and now was experiencing as a 24 year old.

As a dishwasher, I cared about producing a quality product (clean dishes available to the waitresses when they needed them). I also cared about building positive relationships with the kitchen crew, the dining room staff, and the owners. I wanted to be part of the Marshlands Inn family.

Working within the postal outlets felt much the same: I worked to exceed expectations. I trained my outlets to be knowledgeable and responsive. Building relationships that enabled learning was central. Since I was only in a store for two weeks or less, I worked to create connection with other trainers and the management team. A sense of community and intimacy was important to me.

The meaning in your work will fuel your passion. Where there is meaning, there is also a spark to ignite the passion within.

> *"Want to wow people? Flash 'em your passion!"*
> Susan Macaulay, SheQuotes.com

② *Frame for Progress: Start with Action and Notice Success*

Forward movement is critical.

To fuel and sustain your passion, you need to create a sense of movement—forward movement. Human beings were not meant to stand still—when we move our bodies, we feel better; when we take small steps to tackle a big problem, we are more optimistic; when we see tangible results from actions we've taken toward meaningful goals and aspirations, we are uplifted.

Take one step toward something that matters to you each day. Forget magnitude—simply take an action to create some forward movement. Doing this every day will create a momentum that will carry you toward your goals. Taking a 10-minute walk today will build momentum for a 15-minute walk tomorrow, which will, in turn, build momentum for a 20-minute walk next week, and so on. Before you know it, you're fit! Small, consistent steps create forward movement and results.

Forward movement represents progress.

Forward movement tells us we are on track; we are getting somewhere. It affirms we are a life force working wonders in the world—small wonders are still wonders. Beauty embodies the small and the majestic without prejudice.

We often diminish our accomplishments, measuring them by internal or external standards designed to keep us in self-doubt. This does not serve us well. Celebrating our achievements, big or small, bolsters our spirit and helps us navigate life's ups and downs as we journey toward our life goals.

Our final destination is undoubtedly important, but this does not negate the critical role of milestones. As we measure and validate our progress along the way, we build momentum. We feel encouraged and satisfied that the journey—not just the destination—matters.

Teach yourself to see progress.

> *"Feed your passion every day to keep it alive. Without maintenance, you fall into a trance of just getting by. Before you know it, you're sitting in bed, eating chocolate, and watching stupid YouTube videos. For me, reading an article, watching a TED™ talk, or walking my dogs feed my passions. It's amazing how small things keep your passion alive."* Laura Klos Sokol, Poland

I became a manager at a relatively young age and quickly discovered how easy it was to focus on the obstacles that mired a project down or the problems that prevented the organization from living up to its potential.

My team and I were working very hard on a change management project and we had high expectations. The CEO asked us to lead a culture change initiative and we were determined to succeed! Over the next couple of years, we brought in change management programs, we developed new ways of connecting the community, and we 'walked the talk' to the best of our ability. Yet, we were faced with obstacles every time we tried to move from theory into practice. It wore us down, especially me. I wanted to see results for all the energy I was burning. I became increasingly frustrated and began to contemplate leaving. I loved my team, but I couldn't stand the snail's pace of change. It was in that experience that I recognized that caring was not enough—it was crucial to feel the momentum and see progress.

As much as my director tried to reassure me that my team was making great progress, it simply was not visible to me. To sustain my passion, I needed to be part of a change process that was dynamic and impactful. In one sense, we did have an impact: we helped a lot of people develop their skills and change their mindsets. I am very proud of what we achieved; however, *I learned that, to sustain my passion, I needed a clearer sense of progress.*

Many years later, I realized I could have learned to celebrate the progress we were making more genuinely and enthusiastically. So often in life we deprive ourselves of the opportunity to appreciate more subtle forward movement, or we are so busy looking for what we expect to see that we miss what is directly before us!

It was easy to see what was wrong or needed fixing—what was much more difficult to see was what was working and what had been accomplished. Cynicism is the easy way out. Seeing what's changed for the better, and learning how to build on it is a much more difficult task. Choosing to see the bright spots will keep your passion alive.

③ Re-focus and Re-frame: Start over

We all lose our way.

Stuff happens. Things don't turn out the way we expect. We lose our focus. We get lost in the chaos.

To restore my passion, I learned to stop and be still. In that stillness, I taught myself to remember what was meaningful about the task, project, event, or relationship in the first place. I have learned to ground myself in this.

Bringing my mind back to focus on what is truly important is instantly rejuvenating and inspiring. When we get pulled away from a sense of meaning, we need to discipline ourselves, and our minds, on why what we are doing matters. As soon as we do this, we will find resolve—and, if we discover it doesn't actually matter, we can free ourselves to move on.

Refocus on meaning.

A few years ago, I arranged for my elderly parents to join my husband, daughter, and me for a day trip to include a matinee performance of a summer play. It was a special outing to celebrate my birthday.

My parents arrived in good time, but I wasn't quite ready so my father offered to take the dog and my daughter for a walk along the beach. It sounded like a good idea.

As I wrapped up my preparations for the day trip, I began to look for my father. He was nowhere to be seen. Time was getting tight—we had an hour drive to the play and we hadn't eaten lunch yet. We went to the beach. No sign of him. We walked down the road. Again, no sign of him. I began to get irritated. We had already purchased the tickets and it was starting to look like we were not going to be able to make the 2:00 p.m. start time. I complained to my mother: "Didn't Dad know we needed to leave? How could he be so careless and lose track of time!?"

I had just about given up on the entire day's plans when Dad suddenly appeared with my dog and daughter over the sand dune. I turned toward him in anger and, as I did, the silhouette of my father holding his granddaughter by the hand struck me sharply and deeply. I suddenly thought, "How lucky am I that my father has lived to know his granddaughter and she to know him."

In that moment, my sense of progress completely changed. It was no longer about the day's agenda; instead it was about witnessing a special moment of connection between my father and my daughter.

It is easy to miss what's most important. Choosing to remember what's most meaningful to you and choosing to see it before your very eyes will create a sense of progress and ultimately sustain your passion.

 *Remember. See. Appreciate.*

Reframe for progress.

We all experience disappointments, especially when expected results fail to materialize. When this happens to me, I choose to reframe for progress. I ask myself some key questions: What has been gained by this experience? What have I learned? What has been accomplished, regardless of how modest?

As soon as we reframe for a sense of progress, we will feel our resilience return. We have not wasted our time and energy.

We have progressed or we have learned something that will inform future decisions. We then can rest assured that we continue to move forward and grow.

In this realization, we become stronger and more resilient—our passion returns.

Success Strategies

① Always identify what is *meaningful* for you in each of your undertakings.

② As you take action, watch things unfold and see whatever *progress* is there to be seen.

③ As you move forward, take time to *celebrate*. Celebration underscores what is meaningful and highlights progress.

④ Where there is meaning and progress, there is *passion*. Choosing to locate meaning and choosing to see progress will give you a passion-infused life.

Notes

J.L. (Jani) Ashmore

Jani is an international speaker, facilitator, and consultant to corporations in North America, Europe, and Asia Pacific. She helps executives to front-line employees in leadership, sales, customer service, communication skills, and team building. She has contributed to thousands of people in hundreds of organizations.

She has been a trainer for such luminaries as Tony Robbins and Jack Canfield. She has accomplished a black-belt in Karate, ran marathons, and proved herself as a fire-walker.

Jani has co-authored two Amazon.com™ best-selling books, *Success Secrets* and *Nothing But Net.* She has also authored *Stop Managing Start Inspiring: Keys for Leaders to Bring Out the Best in Others.*

www.janiashmore.com

SECTION 4: CHAPTER 5

FEARLESS or *FEAR-less?*

by J.L. (Jani) Ashmore

> *"Courage is resistance to fear, mastery of fear - not absence of fear."* Mark Twain

I t was the 1950's in a rural area of northeastern Colorado. Our farm was small in comparison to many in our dryland farming community. My father rented the land from his father, built a small three-bedroom house for our family of six and, after moving us in, began to build the dairy farming business —the foundation of support for our family for decades to come.

One of my earliest memories includes being a toddler in a highchair at dinner time. I was frightened at seeing a stranger's face in the window and tried to get some family member's attention, but failed to be heard or seen in the effort. This felt like a repeating pattern during my young life—too small to be heard or seen or valued in comparison to all those other family members who were bigger, older, louder, and seemed to always have more privileges (i.e. in my mind, they mattered more).

I was afraid of many things as a youth: the dark; thunder, lightning, and strong winds; threatening clouds; snakes, spiders, and rodents; large animals like horses and cows; not getting my share of food at the table; heights; strangers; new places; trying new things; speaking up; not mattering; embarrassing myself and others; getting lost and losing my parents; what the future might bring. Few of you will relate to these fears and some of you will find them humorous, but this one was my biggest: the fear of falling in the hole of the outhouse and not being seen or heard from again. Sounds funny? Not to a small child! What a relief it was to get our first indoor toilet when I was six. At least that one fear was eliminated early!

I remember my Dad educating me about lightning. He showed me how to count from the time lightning struck the ground until the thunder was heard to determine how far away the lightning was. He was teaching me to use reasoning and to get perspective—two valuable lessons in dealing with fear.

When I was afraid of the dark, my mom taught me to pray. Praying, in and of itself, can strengthen one's faith—another valuable tool when overcome with fear. The other thing it does is keep the mind from continuing to make up stories or expand on the one story it is stuck on telling you over and over. My story was that there was 'something' that was going to come get me in the dark of the night as I lay in bed. Prayer (which is truly a form of meditation) eased my mind into a sense of peace and my body into relaxation so I could fall asleep.

There seemed to be no option but to learn at a very young age that if I was going to have a space to fill on this earth, I'd better start moving past some of those fears or I was never going to count enough to be seen or heard or make a difference. Compared to where I stand in my life now, there is nothing someone could have told that little girl back then to make her believe that her life would turn out the way it has.

What fears did you grow up with and what is your current limiting fear? Are you dealing with fears related to your or a loved one's job, health, relationship, the current state of the world? When have you let fear stop you? What experiences can you recall where you moved through fear anyway and can now draw upon that experience to further your growth and expansion?

There are principles we can all lean on—maybe not to become FEARLESS, but to allow us to be FEAR-less...to not let the fear stop us on our journey through life. It is human nature to have fears, but it is a choice whether or not we let the fears stop us or we work to minimize them and move forward in life.

Was it my knees knocking...or opportunity?

> *"Everything you want is on the other side of fear."*
> *Jack Canfield*

Early in my career, while working at a large corporation, I had to speak in front of a group of 50+ people as part of a regional meeting. As I spoke, I was grateful to be standing in front of a podium. My knees were knocking together so hard, I was afraid the audience would hear them whacking against one another! My stomach churned and my heart pounded. I was light-headed and it seemed my being was somewhere outside my body. Amazingly, these same physical sensations were present the first time I jumped (with a parachute on my back) out of a perfectly good airplane! I know...sounds crazy, but it was one of those things I thought would cure my fear of heights. It didn't. But it did give me a valuable reference point.

If I could complete something I was that afraid of doing, what else might I do that fear was stopping me from accomplishing?

When I finished my talk, I wasn't sure I had made sense. I was glad to hear positive remarks and thanks when I finished, but they paled in comparison to the physical and emotional effects of what it took to make it through that first talk. Similarly, knowing I safely parachuted and landed, hearing the cheers and congratulations, seemed to pale in comparison to the feelings and emotions that still lingered and that I had to overcome to jump out of that plane.

It took continued courage and heart to allow myself to repeat and improve my speaking experiences to achieve the confidence I eventually acquired to now speak in front of groups as part of my passion, purpose, and career.

Believe it or not, after 30 years, I sometimes experience nervousness before a talk...especially a new one. But learning to focus on the five keys in this chapter to moving beyond the fear has supported me in continuing this life process. Did I continue to parachute out of planes? No! Once was enough for me. However, I did tandem skydive once later, which was much less scary for me and much more fun. But parachuting was a good lesson in moving beyond my fears, just not one I chose to repeat! Speaking, however, remains a passion for me.

Where can FEAR-less-ness lead?

My own practices of reducing my fears have allowed me to experience much more in my life than that fearful little girl growing up on the farm could have ever imagined. If someone had told her then where she would travel, what she would see, what she would experience, she could not have believed it.

It has been the building of my library of fear-transcended references that has supported me in continuing to move beyond the fears that pop up in my life. If I have no occasional fear in my life, it usually means I am not taking any risks.

Of course, each person needs to determine the level of risk at which they are willing to play in life.

At whatever level you like to play, there will always be fears that get in the way. The techniques I use to deal with fear are the same ones everyone can use regardless of the degree of risk they want to take.

Here are some of the benefits that were a result of my being willing to move through the fears that could have kept me from experiencing the fulfilling life I have lived to date and the love I've shared with others: I have traveled to over 32 countries; got married and got divorced; walked on fire; moved from my hometown and home state of Colorado to California; swam in the rainforest with piranhas; gave birth to and raised a child that grew into the most amazing woman; ingested a sacred tea that has been used as a healing medicine in the jungles for thousands of years; achieved a black belt in Tae Kwan Do; ran the San Francisco marathon; white-water rafted; co-authored two Amazon.com best-selling books as well as authored a book on my own; stood at the base of a volcano and watched hot molten lava run between the rocks beneath my feet; took a trapeze class with my granddaughter; bent rebar at my neck; survived surgery on the trunk of my body; sent my child off to school and then college; bought/sold a house on my own; parachuted and tandem skydived out of an airplane; started a new business multiple times; and sat with family members as they made their transition from this life to the next.

And in the end ...

> *"If you can't, you must!"*
> *Tony Robbins*

Some of you read this quote and rebel against it, saying, "I can't and I won't!" It is always your CHOICE. Helen Keller said, "Life is a daring adventure or nothing!" I may like the daring part, but there are many levels in between all and nothing.

You will need to find your desired level of playing the game of life—somewhere in that vast space between 'all' and 'nothing.' And you need to know that your fulfillment might be just on the other side of whatever fear you are letting stop you.

Marianne Williamson, in *A Return to Love: Reflections on the Principles of 'A Course in Miracles'* says: "Our deepest fear is not that we are inadequate. Our deepest fear is that we are powerful beyond measure. It is our light, not our darkness, that most frightens us. We ask ourselves, 'Who am I to be brilliant, gorgeous, talented, fabulous?' Actually, who are you *not* to be? You are a child of God. Your playing small does not serve the world. There is nothing enlightened about shrinking so that other people won't feel insecure around you. We are all meant to shine, as children do. We were born to make manifest the glory of God that is within us. It's not just in some of us; it's in everyone. And as we let our own light shine, we unconsciously give other people permission to do the same. As we are liberated from our own fear, our presence automatically liberates others."

Go ahead...take a leap and see what's on the other side of that fear! To help you, the following are five of my favorite techniques to deal with fear.

Five Keys to Being FEAR-less

 *Life Purpose*

> *"When I dare to be powerful, to use my strength in the service of my vision, then it becomes less and less important whether I am afraid."* Audre Lorde

When we know our purpose in life, there is a pull, a strength that can help move us beyond our fears. Purpose gives direction and a reason that can surpass the fear.

When we are clear about our purpose—and understand that our fulfillment depends on it—we can draw from the well of inspiration, motivation, and courage to deal with the fear.

My purpose to inspire others inspires me.

② *Education*

> *"Nothing in life is to be feared. It is only to be understood. Now is the time to understand more, so that we may fear less."* Marie Curie

Information is education and it can bring us a new perspective with which to reason.

My Dad taught me that 80% to 90% of lightning is far away. So, 80% to 90% of the time, my fear was lessened. With knowledge, we can focus on the unreasonableness of our fears and identify when our fears are affecting our health, or our ability to move forward.

 *Commitment*

> *"Courage does not always roar like a lion. Sometimes it is a quiet voice at the end of the day that says, 'I will try again tomorrow.'" Peter Sheridan*

Commitment does not have to be fierce and unrelenting. It can be as gentle as a spring rain that is persistent over time and can build enough water to be as powerful as a deluge that happens in only minutes. With clarity of purpose and the belief and faith that we are on the right track, commitment naturally presents itself in the moment.

Fear comes from the mind; commitment from the body, the heart. That shift from head to heart knocks fear...right up the side of the head!

 *Belief/Faith*

> *"Faith is the flame that eliminates fear."*
> *Suzy Kassem*

What are your beliefs that are manifesting the fears? What are the beliefs that will melt the fears away?

A belief is a thought we keep having over and over again until we no longer question the thought. It becomes what we then call a belief. Think a different thought—one that will alleviate the fear. That thought can become a belief as well: one that will empower versus one that is dis-empowering.

References

> *"Whether you think you can or think you can't – you're right."* Henry Ford, Founder Ford Motor Company

At times, looking at our past can help us move into our future. Fears may be mounting, but are they new fears or 'old friends' who are popping up again? You may find that the fear holding you back now is one you already conquered, and all you need is a reminder.

Develop a 'victory list' that you can refer to whenever the need arises. Start by making a list of 100 of your accomplishments. Don't make a judgment as to how large or small the accomplishment—it could be as large as asking your boss for a raise or as small (in retrospect) as stepping onto the bus on your first day of school.

Indicate any fears you experienced with each of those accomplishments.

Each time you face a fear and move through it, add it to your victory list. Refer back to your 'library' of fear-conquered references when you require some support to overcome the next fear you need to address in life.

Using these five keys has allowed me to overcome fears and difficulties and unlock the door to my successful life. Put fear it its place, and you, too, can live the life of your dreams!

There are many techniques to deal with fear. Following are a few of my favorites:

1. *Self-talk* happens in the form of contemplation, prayer, affirmations, and awareness training.

2. *Positive Habits* that help to calm our fears may include journaling, reading inspirational literature, or exercising to move the fear-based energy.

3. *Emotional Freedom Technique (EFT)* is a method that helps clear energetic blockages from our body. EFT can dramatically reduce fears and phobias. See *www.thetappingsolution.com.*

4. *Transformational Breathing* is another method that can help alleviate fear. It is a technique that can transform the fear energy in your body and replace it with peace, joy, and love. See *www.transformationalbreath.com.*

5. *Visualization* can be a valuable technique for dealing with fear. It may take focus and imagination to change the story your mind is viewing, but it can be a fun way to alleviate fear. Add sound and especially feeling for the most effective visualizations.

Anita Sanchez

Anita is a brilliant leadership coach, consultant, and trainer who works with women and men in business, non-profits and education all over the world.

Author of ***Discovering Your Positive Core – A Personal Guide***®, Anita is renowned for her work in leadership, diversity and inclusion, cultures of engagement, and positive change. Her passion is bridging indigenous wisdom and the latest in science to inspire and equip women to live their higher purpose in service and joy.

Anita is a member of the Transformational Leadership Council and serves as a Board Member for Bioneers. She lives in the mountains above Boulder, Colorado, with her family.

www.SanchezTennis.com
www.anitasanchezmeditations.com

SECTION 4: CHAPTER 6

Entering the Heart of Reality - Spirituality

by Anita Sanchez

> *"We cultivate love when we allow our most vulnerable and powerful selves to be deeply seen and known, and when we honor the spiritual connection that grows from that offering with trust, respect, kindness and affection." Brene Brown*

Soaring Like an Eagle

*T*here is a huge, deep well of joy in my life and a large well of pain. Do you have a well of joy? Do you have a well of pain? There were times in my life when I believed and acted "as if" my well of pain was much larger than my well of joy—it felt as if my joy was almost non-existent in comparison to my pain. With a belief in spiritual connection— that all life is sacred and all life is connected—and an active practice of acknowledging our spiritual connection through positive action, I now know my well of joy is infinite in size. I am open to receive and I know how to create joy and success in my life. Shining my inner light and holding the mirror up so other women can clearly see their sacredness, their connection to all life, to receive and to share their gifts is an ennobling life service for me.

One example of positive action grounded from spiritual connection is the story of how I was able to finally write my doctoral dissertation, no longer making everyone and everything else more important. Maybe some of you are good at procrastination or putting lower-level priorities first. Well, I painted everything in my house including the kitchen cabinets, which took four months, in order to avoid writing that dissertation.

In spite of many real barriers in my life including economic poverty, childhood sexual abuse, death of a parent, race and gender discrimination, I felt that I had already accomplished so much, done so many good things in my life, and would continue to do so. So I thought to myself, "Do I really need to have a doctoral degree?"

With no more house painting to do, I got angry, crying and screaming at God, Grandmother, and Grandfather. I said, "Why are you making me do this doctorate? I am tired. I will continue to do good in the world even if I don't get this degree. I still promise to be about social change: I am not going to abandon my work of advocating for those who do not have access, advocating for justice, for the rights of people and nature. Women and people of all races will still get my attention. With others, I will create environments where life can thrive—where each of us can contribute our gifts and receive gifts."

As I stood on my back deck overlooking the Continental Divide—a row of snow-covered peaks—I continued, "Okay,

God, Grandmother, and Grandfather: if you want me to write this dissertation, then you must give me a sign. Yes, you give me a clear sign that this is what you want me to do." I gave them this ultimatum and for a split second thought to myself, "Thank goodness the weather is clear. Wouldn't want lightning to strike me; no chance of that on this clear day."

That was the end of that—no more need to avoid writing and I could go on with my life. As I stood there deepening my breath, hoarse from screaming and through drying tears on my face, not one, but two, beautiful golden eagles majestically danced in flight, together. As they caught the updraft coming next to my deck and rocks beyond, I could count the talons on their feet; make out the specific color and design of their feathers. For a split second, I believed that I caught a piercing glimpse of their eyes.

This scene of one, let alone two, eagles flying within 12 feet of my upstairs windows and deck is not a common occurrence. Those eagles were not looking for a meal or prey below in the canyon. Those eagles were here for me. I looked up and shouted, "Okay, God, here is the deal: I will write my dissertation as long as this is really what I am supposed to do. Every morning I will arise at five o'clock. I will look west out on the Continental Divide, and if an eagle flies by, then I will go to my desk and write for three hours."

The most miraculous events happened. Yes, every day for the next three months, I got up and went to the window or stood out on the deck...and, sure enough, an eagle (sometimes two) soared by and I proceeded to my desk to write from 5:00 a.m. to 8:00 a.m.

Some days the writing flowed; other days writing meant holding up my head as I stared at the computer and the view out my window. Regardless of the number of pages or words I wrote, I dutifully sat at my desk and dared not rise from my chair until the three hours had passed.

Admittedly, I did get a little perturbed at these eagle guides. Having written for three hours, I would ascend the stairs while enjoying the beauty of the morning and make my breakfast. Peacefully eating my morning meal and planning my work day, I thought, "What else will I do today?" If my plans were thwarted, I would say, "Oh, no, not you again," to the eagle with its gorgeous, powerful wings as it swooped by the window. My eagle guides were not taking 'no' for an answer; the eagles were not accepting any procrastination from fulfilling my current journey in life. "Alright," I would say to the guide. Grabbing my mug of herbal tea, I returned to the office for another three hours of writing.

Every day, I grew more and more appreciative of my connection to these magnificent birds that came to inspire me to stay on the path to complete my dissertation. In three months, the complete draft was ready for my committee chair to review. My eagle guides (surely sent by God, Grandmother, Grandfather, the universe) miraculously held the space for me to write, *"The Contribution of Personality Preference, Organizational, and Situational Variables to Visionary Leadership Behavior,"* by Anita L. Sanchez, PhD., drawing from a 43-country sample of women executives in YWCAs.

Today, I know to trust my inner spirit and universal spiritual connection. The eagles, nature, and human beings (friends, foes, colleagues, bosses, and strangers) are all related. We can joyfully fulfill our higher purpose and care for all our relations.

When I am grounded in this spiritual awareness, I know I am sacred (all beings are sacred) and I am uniquely me; we are all One. Now, my conscious journey is filled with positive actions that create and honor life. Joy and success are an inevitable part of life and one of the greatest joys in life is to be in search of one thing and to discover another.

On my spiritual journey I've come to realize that trying to plan and control everything is one of the ways that you and I have robbed ourselves of the joy of living our miraculous power of spiritual connection.

> *"In search of my mother's garden I found my own."*
> *Alice Walker*

The pure joyfulness of the unexpected continues to be a source of wonder to me. And so it was as my family and I prepared for our first journey into the heart of everything: *Ecuador.*

Preparing for the Journey of a Lifetime

Some of our best work, using positive psychology and the power of appreciative inquiry, had been completed at Hewlett-Packard Company. Thousands of men and women had been inspired and connected to thousands of their colleagues and leaders around the world. The ignited leadership, at all levels, had grown one of their business units from $26 billion to $30 billion in revenue during a down market. The financial reward to the company had been great that year, and the light that was lit inside of their people and throughout their networks was even greater than those billions of dollars could indicate.

It was also a year of some powerful professional and personal development for me where I deepened trust in the light within me and light connecting all beings. As one of 18 members of a year-long global leadership circle, we challenged and lovingly supported each other to be whole spiritual beings in human form and to do what was best for self and communities around the world. As a way to extend our connection and deepen our understanding of who we were, individually and collectively on this earth, Lynne Twist, the Co-Founder of the Pachamama Alliance, planned a private journey for members of our global circle to journey into the heart of the world during the next year. We were to travel to the small country of Ecuador, which contains more bio-diversity than any other place on earth. The trip was scheduled for August. I felt strongly that my entire family should take this journey together and, because my sons would be in school, I declined.

Several months later, Lynne wrote to our global circle members apologizing that the journey would be postponed. The new dates would be December 28, 2007 to January 8, 2008. This special journey would coincide with ownership of the Kapawi Eco-lodge being turned over to the Achuar, the ancient, local indigenous tribe. It would be a great celebration for the Achuar and other tribes throughout South America. Kapawi would be the first eco-lodge not only operated by indigenous people, but also owned by them. "Yes!" I shouted. Kit, my husband, and I immediately wrote and said that we wanted four spots on the journey for us and our two sons, Alex, 16, and Nico, 11. "I can't tell you how it will impact each of us, but my waking and sleeping dreams tell me this is going to be a most powerful, life-changing journey for each of us."

There was a lot to prepare for this journey, including special equipment and clothes for our trek in the rainforest; many inoculations to prevent exotic diseases; and phone calls to begin creating community with the other 14 travelers and local guides. It was fun as we immersed ourselves in the history, culture, ceremony, and stories of the Achuar People and their pristine lands in the heart of the rainforest, at the beginning of the uppermost reaches of the Amazon.

Evenings were spent reading aloud with Nico, who declared he would only read one of the nine books on the Pachamama

Recommended Reading List. His choice was *Ishmael* by Daniel Quinn. Alex made it clear that he did not have time to read, "I should do my real homework. I am going with the family, but it doesn't mean that I will like it." Oh, how his attitude and behavior changed during the journey—but that is another story of spiritual connection.

Kit and I pored over the other books. The photos and stories were an exploration into a seemingly separate, different world—a dream-based culture with fierce warriors, women and men, living as part of nature.

While reading Joe Kane's book, *Savages*, I imagined being in their place, an Achuar. I shouted with delight as tears came to my eyes, "Kit, come here. Read this. Read this!" Kit responded, "Anita, it's a book. You don't have to scream as if your life depended on it." "But, you'll see. It is about our life and the indigenous people who we have never met," I said impatiently. "Sit here," pointing to the space next to me on the couch, and I began to read: "DuPont's CEO, Edgar Woolard, had made it known that he would not give Conoco the go-ahead for its Oriente project unless the oil company came up with some sort of "green" blessing—some stamp. The indigenous people of the local tribes must sign a letter that they agree to this oil development. The Huarani, the local tribe, did not recognize the outside groups who were trying to speak for them.

There were signs from earlier exploration that the Indians suffered most from the consequences of oil development... DuPont's Edgar Woolard had yet to decide whether he would allow Conoco, a subsidiary of DuPont, to proceed with developing Block Sixteen, and the meeting held at the Capuchin mission the day before had been another bid by Conoco to win the stamp of approval Woolard required."

Kit, anxious for the news, jumped in, "Okay, how did the meeting turn out?" I enthusiastically read, "Edgar S. Woolard,

Chairman, of DuPont. Letter to NRDC, October 18, 1990. Amazon Oil Exploration Suspended."

Kit smiled from ear to ear, as he exhaled a great sigh of relief.

"The story of local tribes and rainforest in Ecuador is, in part, our story, too. Kit, you and I, along with our colleagues, played a part in educating the leaders in DuPont to respect and preserve cultures and people. Could it be?" Tears in our eyes, Kit and I gazed at each other. I spoke softly, "Life is miraculous! Fifteen years after the CEO of DuPont decided not to do oil drilling in Ecuador, we will now meet face to face with the Achuar whose lives and lands were saved. They probably already know that we have been working on each other's behalf, on the behalf of life itself. We are all connected; we are so fortunate to be reminded."

Each of us has magical moments in our lives when we become awakened to the oneness of all things. When that happens, we see the "motions and patterns and connections," as Jean Houston would say. A feeling of warmth permeates our being and we breathe a breath of heartfelt relief. We can know the unknowable; we do know the unknowable.

Luckily, living life fully is not a task. It is an opportunity to enter and live in the heart of reality, soaring like an eagle. When we learn to trust our own perceptions and experiences—spiritual as well as earthly—we discover that we begin to have a relationship with the process of the universe. In fact, we are living out of our own process; we are one with the universe.

This living process that is us is, at the same time, greater than ourselves. When we are truly ourselves, we are more than ourselves. We do not have to *look* for spirituality, we *are* spirituality.

Our spirituality is much more all-encompassing than many of us care to admit. Everything we do flows from ourselves as spiritual beings: making decisions, interacting at work, doing the dishes, caring for children ....

When we stop removing our spiritual selves from our daily selves we recognize that all we do is spiritual, that all life is connected.

Success Strategies

1. Know that you are a *spiritual being.*

2. Recognize that *inspiration, spirit,* is ever present in our work and life.

3. *Soar like an eagle* - don't be afraid to ask for guidance.

4. *Connect to your breath* - breathing is the first locus of control used to attain higher levels of self awareness, self management, and spiritual connection to self and others.

5. Become *conscious* of how you use your energy - what are you giving your attention to each day?

6. Explore and embrace the *traditional* indigenous and growing scientific world view that we are all related, all connected.

Success!

Congratulations
GRADUATE!

To obtain your Certificate of Achievement, please email us at *certificate@successuniversityforwomen.com* with the word 'Certificate' in the subject line. We'll email you your Certificate and keep you up-to-date on upcoming events in *Success University for Women*™.

CERTIFICATE OF ACHIEVEMENT

WISDOM WORKING FOR YOU

LEVEL ONE

You have successfully completed Level One
of the *Success University for Women*™ curriculum.
You have taken your FIRST steps towards achieving
greater SUCCESS and JOY in your life!

Co-Founders, *Success University for Women*™

Jan Fraser

Catherine Scheers

Success University for Women™

Success University for Women™ *Curriculum*

Want more success in your life? Now that you've finished this book (Level One of our 'curriculum'), keep the momentum going with *Success University for Women*™ Conferences, *Success University for Women*™ **Companion Workbooks,** online courses, and upcoming volumes.

Success University for Women™ *Conferences*

Need a motivational 'shot-in-the-arm' or a 'kick in your determination?' Want to meet the co-creators of *Success University for Women*™ and connect with the authors? You won't want to miss the rewarding *Success University for Women*™ Conferences. Held in exciting cities around the world, these conferences bring together our authors and readers— women who will inspire and uplift you and help you to succeed in life! You'll benefit from keynote speakers, breakout working sessions, and networking with wise women from around the world!

Success University for Women™ *Conference Calendar*

Check our website for upcoming dates and locations: *www.successuniversityforwomen.com*

Success University for Women™

Success University for Women™ *Invitation*

Do you want to be an author in an upcoming *Success University for Women*™ book? Are you a successful woman creating success ripples and have an inspirational message to share with the world?

Contact us at *submit@successuniversityforwomen.com* with the words 'SUW Writer Proposal' in the subject line to share your inspiring success stories. You may become a contributor in one of our upcoming volumes.

Made in the USA
Coppell, TX
23 July 2021

59392577R10184